Australian Westerns in the Fifties

Derham Groves

Australian Westerns in the Fifties

Kangaroo, Hopalong Cassidy on Tour, and *Whiplash*

Derham Groves
Faculty of Architecture, Bldg & Planning
University of Melbourne
Melbourne, VIC, Australia

ISBN 978-3-031-12882-0   ISBN 978-3-031-12883-7 (eBook)
https://doi.org/10.1007/978-3-031-12883-7

© The Editor(s) (if applicable) and The Author(s), under exclusive licence to Springer Nature Switzerland AG 2022
This work is subject to copyright. All rights are solely and exclusively licensed by the Publisher, whether the whole or part of the material is concerned, specifically the rights of translation, reprinting, reuse of illustrations, recitation, broadcasting, reproduction on microfilms or in any other physical way, and transmission or information storage and retrieval, electronic adaptation, computer software, or by similar or dissimilar methodology now known or hereafter developed.
The use of general descriptive names, registered names, trademarks, service marks, etc. in this publication does not imply, even in the absence of a specific statement, that such names are exempt from the relevant protective laws and regulations and therefore free for general use.
The publisher, the authors, and the editors are safe to assume that the advice and information in this book are believed to be true and accurate at the date of publication. Neither the publisher nor the authors or the editors give a warranty, expressed or implied, with respect to the material contained herein or for any errors or omissions that may have been made. The publisher remains neutral with regard to jurisdictional claims in published maps and institutional affiliations.

This Palgrave Macmillan imprint is published by the registered company Springer Nature Switzerland AG.
The registered company address is: Gewerbestrasse 11, 6330 Cham, Switzerland

In memory of Lorraine Callander (1944–2022)

PREFACE

I was born in 1956—the same year television arrived in Australia—so I grew up watching lots of American Westerns on TV, such as *Hopalong Cassidy* (1952–1954), *Gunsmoke* (1955–1975), *The Life and Legend of Wyatt Earp* (1955–1961), *Tales of the Texas Rangers* (1955–1959), *Have Gun Will Travel* (1957–1963), *Tales of Wells Fargo* (1957–1962), *Wagon Train* (1957–1965), *Bat Masterson* (1958–1961), and *Bonanza* (1959–1973). As kids, my friends and I played "cowboys and Indians" at home and school, armed with cap guns and bows and suction-cup arrows and wearing cowboy hats and Indian headdresses, all purchased from the corner toyshop. One of my favourite children's books was *The Indians and Cowboys Book* (1962) by Kathryn Jackson (1907–1985) and Byron Jackson (1899–1949) and illustrated by Gustaf Tenggren (1896–1970), which I still own (Fig. 1). Although, I suspect hardly any Australian children play cowboys and Indians nowadays. Travelling on a Melbourne tram recently, I saw a five-year-old boy playfully make a gun with his thumb and forefinger. 'We don't do that anymore,' his 30-something father told him rather sternly!

While American Westerns were all the rage following World War II, they had a certain sameness that prompted some movie and television producers to look for different ways to freshen up the popular but "tired" genre. Since most were filmed 'within 30 miles of Hollywood and a lot of that scenery is becoming mighty familiar,' according to one Hollywood insider, some filmmakers decided that a change of scenery might do the trick. "Spaghetti Westerns" made in Europe, such as *A Fist Full of Dollars*

Fig. 1 *The Indians and Cowboys Book* (1962) by Kathryn and Byron Jackson

(1964), *The Good, the Bad, and the Ugly* (1966), and *Once Upon a Time in the West* (1967) are well known. On the other hand, "Meat Pie Westerns" made in Australia that pre-date Spaghetti Westerns are less known.

Australian Westerns in the Fifties is the second Palgrave Pivot book I've written. I enjoy the discipline imposed by the series' 50,000-word limit, which is long enough to study a subject in depth but requires a focused outlook. So, while the book is not exhaustive, I believe it is representative. Chapter 1 looks at *Kangaroo: The Australian Story* (1952). It was a big-budget Australian Western film set and made in Australia by a top American motion picture studio at the beginning of the 1950s, starring leading Hollywood performers and aimed at an adult audience. Chapter 2 looks at Hopalong Cassidy's goodwill tour of Australia in 1954. It illustrates the popularity of cowboys and Westerns with Australian baby boomers and the rise and importance of TV merchandising. Finally, Chap. 3 looks at *Whiplash* (1960–1961). It was a big-budget Australian Western TV series set and made in Australia by a top British TV production company at the end of the 1950s, starring a leading Hollywood actor supported by leading Australian performers and aimed at families. Some common threads run between the three chapters of the book, such as the authority of overseas production companies, the presence of Hollywood actors, encounters with First Nations Australians, etc. Also, post-World War II Australian monetary policy prompted both the making of *Kangaroo* and the visit by Hopalong Cassidy. Before becoming *Kangaroo*'s assistant director, Nate Watt (1889–1968) directed several Hopalong Cassidy Westerns. The use of whips as weapons in *Kangaroo* inspired their similar use in *Whiplash*. Several members of the cast and crew of *Kangaroo* and *Whiplash* worked on the American TV Western *Have Gun Will Travel*. There are many crossovers.

In the 1950s, Australian Westerns were different from American Westerns, which I attribute mainly to the influence of place. Some of the plainest differences, for example, were Aboriginals instead of Native Americans, the bush instead of the prairie, Cobb & Co. instead of Wells Fargo, kangaroos instead of bison, and stockmen instead of cowboys. There were also less evident factors of significance, such as accommodation, remoteness, and the weather. Therefore, I not only look at place but also process, context, and chance. While taking a phenomenological approach to the subject seemed like the obvious way to go to me, surprisingly, few others have done so. Furthermore, because the main participants were sharp-eyed outsiders—Hollywood performers and overseas filmmakers—a unique picture emerges through the retelling of their stories of everyday life and the film and television industry in Australia during the 1950s.

Brunswick West, VIC, Australia   Derham Groves
May 2022

About This Book

The week I write this, the most popular Western in the world is probably the music video for "That That," a song by cheeky South Korean rapper PSY, featuring SUGA of the K-Pop group BTS. Within a week of its release, it collected over 100 million views online. A posse of synchronised dancers in surreal fringe bring Korean hip-hop to a Western film set (Fig. 2). This is the latest in a long line of K-Pop Western shorts over the past decade, including BTS's own "Permission to Dance" (2021). In a different register, at the 94th Academy Awards in March 2022, the most prominent Western was *The Power of the Dog*, for which writer and director Jane Campion won Best Director. Campion is from Aotearoa/New Zealand, and the film was shot in the Otago region, standing in for the story's Montana. Today's fictional frontier is not your grandfather's Western. Or is it?

As Derham Groves shows us in this delightful book, the 1950s—the decade known as a Golden Age of Hollywood Westerns in the USA—witnessed a flourishing of Westerns across the Dateline and Down Under from Hollywood. On the big screen (in *Kangaroo*), on the small screen (in *Whiplash*), and in person (in Hopalong Cassidy on Tour), Australia was the setting for a fictional West parallel to and yet distinct from the North American variety. Drawing on the continent's bush landscape, its Indigenous peoples, and its history of settler colonialism, the "Meat Pie Western" appears here as central to a genre that has in fact been global since its very beginnings.

Fig. 2 "That That" by PSY and featuring SUGA of BTS

In 1875, well before Buffalo Bill Cody sailed the ocean blue with his Wild West crew, German writer Karl May debuted his indelible character Winnetou, the Apache blood brother of the frontiersman Old Shatterhand. In 1906, just three years after the supposed first Western film, the 12-minute *Great Train Robbery*, and four years after the classic American novel *The Virginian*, Australians produced *The Story of the Kelly Gang*. This was arguably the first feature-length "Western" film. By the 1950s and 1960s, the imagined West was being shaped by youth gangs in Kinshasa (Leopoldville) in the Belgian Congo who wore cowboy clothes and called themselves "Bills" after Buffalo Bill, by Israeli pulp novelists narrating the Hebrew tales of Buk G'ons (aka Buck Jones), and by the blockbuster Czech parody *Lemonade Joe, or the Horse Opera*. In the 1970s, Hungarian longhorn grey cattle grazed the cinematic Eastern European Plains; bandits stalked trains in the Indian epic film *Sholay*; and Bob Marley sang "I Shot the Sheriff" and "Buffalo Soldier" in Jamaica.[1]

The Western genre is quintessentially American. And yet, like the real American West, it has exchanged ingredients with the rest of the world for a very long time. In Spaghetti Westerns, Goulash Westerns, Masala Westerns, and Ramen Westerns, and here in Meat Pie Westerns, a smorgasbord of stories explore heroes, villains, war, peace, adventure, and dramatic landscapes the world over. (We'll leave the subject of Space Westerns for another time, though do note in this book how *Star Trek* creator Gene

Roddenberry ventured first to the tales of *Whiplash* before he discovered his final frontier.) Derham captures evocatively the way Australians, Americans, and others came together to produce new versions of the West in mid-century Oz.

Josh Garrett-Davis
Gamble Associate Curator of Western History
Popular Culture, and Firearms
Autry Museum of the American West, Los Angeles
May 2022

NOTE

1. See Rachel Leket-Mor, "IsraPulp: The Israeli Popular Literature Collection at Arizona State University," *Judaica Librarianship* 16 (2011), 1–53; Ch. Didier Gondola, *Tropical Cowboys: Westerns, Violence, and Masculinity in Kinshasa* (Bloomington: Indiana University Press, 2016); and Cynthia J. Miller and A. Bowdoin Van Riper, eds. *International Westerns: Re-Locating the Frontier* (Lanham, MD: Scarecrow Press, 2014).

Contents

1	**Kangaroo: The Australian Story**	1
	The Producers	2
	The Script	5
	The Stars	8
	The Story	14
	Woolundunga	19
	Heat, Willy-Willies, and Flies	24
	Terra Nullius	26
	Zanuckville	32
	The Critics	37
2	Hopalong Cassidy on Tour	49
	Darwin Airport	50
	Darwin Schools	55
	Royal Children's Hospital	63
	Yooralla	66
	Victorian School for Deaf Children	68
	Wirth's Circus	70
	Merchandising	76
	So Long, Pardner	84

3 **Whiplash**   91
   The American Star   92
   The Graveses in Australia   97
   The Writers   101
   The Producers   105
   The Actors and Actresses   110
   Presenting Aboriginal Culture   114
   Danger!   120
   The Horses and Stagecoaches   123
   The Studio and the Set   125
   The Critics   130
   The Author   131

Index   139

List of Figures

Fig. 1.1	Producer Robert Bassler (*left*) and director Lewis Milestone	3
Fig. 1.2	Richard Boone as John W. Gamble (*left*) and Peter Lawford as Richard Connor	10
Fig. 1.3	Maureen O'Hara as Del McGuire on her horse	13
Fig. 1.4	Finlay Currie as Michael McGuire	14
Fig. 1.5	The thirsty Aboriginals meet the McGuires with their thirsty cattle at a water trough	18
Fig. 1.6	John Endean's sketch of Connor and Gamble searching Michael McGuire	19
Fig. 1.7	The homestead built for *Kangaroo* on Woolundunga Station	22
Fig. 1.8	A four-inch double-headed nail	23
Fig. 1.9	George Westenhiser (*right*) spraying Maureen O'Hara with DDT	25
Fig. 1.10	Poster for *Kangaroo* showing marauding kangaroos	29
Fig. 1.11	Zanuckville, Port Augusta, South Australia (c.1950)	32
Fig. 1.12	Miss *Kangaroo*, Loretta North, and Joey	37
Fig. 2.1	William Boyd (*centre*) and the 44 American newspaper boys about to depart for England	51
Fig. 2.2	Two sides of a Hopalong Cassidy good luck token	53
Fig. 2.3	William Boyd (*centre*) and Matthias Ulungura (*right*) at St Mary's Presbytery	58
Fig. 2.4	Royal Children's Hospital staff craning to see Hopalong Cassidy	65
Fig. 2.5	Ben Lewin (*centre*) pointing his toy gun at Hopalong Cassidy	67
Fig. 2.6	Hopalong Cassidy arriving at the Victorian School for Deaf Children	69
Fig. 2.7	William Boyd (*arrow*) calls for calm at Wirth's Circus	74
Fig. 2.8	Hoppy Cola bottle	78

Fig. 2.9	Hopalong Cassidy Game manufactured by W. Owen Pty. Ltd.	79
Fig. 2.10	Hoppy Belt Pouch (*left*) and Hopalong Cassidy Ranch Toffees tin	81
Fig. 2.11	(*Clockwise*) Hopalong Cassidy Vegemite, Tim Tams, sunscreen and boomerang	83
Fig. 3.1	Freeman Cobb (*left*) and Peter Graves as Chris Cobb	93
Fig. 3.2	Chris Cobb and his stockwhip from *Whiplash Painting Book* (n.d.)	95
Fig. 3.3	Houses and shops in Avalon Beach (c.1960)	99
Fig. 3.4	Michael Plant (*left*) and Michael Noonan	101
Fig. 3.5	Peter Graves as Chris Cobb with a koala	105
Fig. 3.6	Bren Brown, Maury Geraghty, Ross Wood, and Bob Wright (*clockwise*)	106
Fig. 3.7	Ken Goodlet as Mick Jacky (*left*) and Anthony Wickert as Dan Ledward	110
Fig. 3.8	Chips Rafferty as Sorrel (*left*) and Peter Graves as Chris Cobb on the set of "The Adelaide Arabs"	113
Fig. 3.9	The Alice Springs Hotel (c.1959)	115
Fig. 3.10	Reg Livermore as Maloomba (*left*) and Peter Graves as Chris Cobb in "The Legacy"	117
Fig. 3.11	Anthony Wickert as Dan Ledward (*left*) and Peter Graves as Chris Cobb driving a stagecoach	125
Fig. 3.12	Workmen constructing Fury Creek (1959)	127
Fig. 3.13	Shops at the Pioneer Settlement, Swan Hill, Victoria (1970s)	129

CHAPTER 1

Kangaroo: The Australian Story

Abstract This chapter is about *Kangaroo: The Australian Story*, the 20th Century Fox Western film set and shot in Australia in 1950. It looks at the twists and turns involved in selecting the film's title, as well as its director, Lewis Milestone. It discusses the changes that were made to the story due to the American filmmakers' ignorance of Australia. It outlines the long-winded process of casting Maureen O'Hara as Del McGuire and Peter Lawford as Richard Connor. It also talks about the film's other performers, including Richard Boone, Finlay Currie, and Chips Rafferty. It describes the design and construction of *Kangaroo*'s main set, the McGuires' homestead. It details the problems caused by making the film during summer in one of the hottest and dustiest places in Australia. It examines the depiction of Aboriginals and their culture. It looks at Zanuckville, the colony built on the outskirts of Port Augusta, South Australia, especially for the cast and crew. Finally, this chapter reviews some of the bizarre stunts employed to publicise *Kangaroo* and the critics' reactions to the film.

Keywords Aboriginals • Australia • Lewis Milestone • Maureen O'Hara • Peter Lawford • Port Augusta • Richard Boone • Zanuckville

© The Author(s), under exclusive license to Springer Nature Switzerland AG 2022
D. Groves, *Australian Westerns in the Fifties*,
https://doi.org/10.1007/978-3-031-12883-7_1

The Producers

In November 1948, the American film studio 20th Century Fox announced plans to make a film called *The Australian Story* about 'the construction of the transcontinental telegraph line'[1] in Australia. Then they changed its name to *The Land Down Under*.[2] Then it was going to be 'about a highwayman in the pioneer days' and called *The Bushranger*.[3] Then they decided to call it *The Sundowner*, saying it 'will not be based on any particular bushranger's life.'[4] Finally, they settled on the title *Kangaroo: The Australian Story*. Talk about being all over the place! Money was the main motivation for the made-in-Australia film (hereafter referred to as *Kangaroo*, but not to be confused with the 1923 novel of the same name by D.H. Lawrence). Following World War II (1939–1945), the Australian government "froze" a percentage of funds earned in Australia by American companies, forcing them to either save it or spend it there. Thus making *Kangaroo* in Australia would release A£210,000 (equivalent to US$475,000) of 'Fox loot earned in that country,'[5] *The Daily News* said. The studio's decision was closely watched by other American film companies 'to see how much they can save in making movies in Australia to determine to what extent they will break into the Australian production field,' *The Sydney Morning Herald* said. 'One of the major reasons for their sudden interest [...] is the devaluation of the Australian pound.'[6] So, making films in Australia not only freed up their frozen funds but also resulted in more bang for their bucks. *Kangaroo*'s press liaison officer was the New Zealand-Australian author, Max Brown (1916–2003), best known for his 1948 biography of the notorious Australian bushranger Ned Kelly (1854–1880).[7] Brown's only novel, *Wild Turkey* (1958), is a fictionalised account of the making of *Kangaroo*. On the subject of "defrosting" frozen funds, he wrote:

> The Commonwealth permitted only 70 per cent of profits to leave the country, hence Colossus [Brown's fictional American film studio], in order to free the frozen 30 per cent for use on some other sector of its world setup, had evolved the formula: 'Australian frozen profits converted into celluloid and multiplied by world distribution equals usable income in American dollars and other foreign currencies.' The alternative was to spend the frozen profits from the pockets of Australians on their behinds—namely on new cinemas. But what did it matter whether Australians sat on foam rubber or on bug benches when America's fourth industry needed every cent to fight television![8]

The head of 20th Century Fox, Daryl F. Zanuck (1902–1979), put Robert Bassler (1903–1975) in charge of making *Kangaroo*. He had started as a film editor, was analytical and creative, and always sought speedy, straightforward solutions, Max Brown said, wearing his publicist's hat.[9] Bassler was responsible for several highly acclaimed films, including the kids-and-horses Western *Green Grass of Wyoming* (1948), which several of the *Kangaroo* filmmakers also worked on. Then he produced the romantic musical *Gentlemen Marry Brunettes* (1955), a huge flop, which virtually ended his film career. Initially, Bassler was also going to direct *Kangaroo*.[10] Then the American Academy Award-winning director Dudley Nichols (1885–1960) was going to do it and write the script.[11] Then Louis King (1898–1962), a Western specialist who also directed *Green Grass of Wyoming*, was going to do it.[12] Finally, the job went to the Russian-American director Lewis Milestone (1895–1980), who had won Academy Awards for the World War I comedy *Two Arabian Knights* (1927), starring William Boyd (1895–1972, see Chap. 2), and the World War I epic *All Quiet on the Western Front* (1930) (Fig. 1.1). Like choosing the film's title, selecting its director was also a "dog's breakfast." According to *The Daily Telegraph*, the appointment of Milestone, 'one of Hollywood's top directors,' showed that *Kangaroo* was one of Zanuck's pet projects.[13] Although perhaps more importantly, Bassler and Milestone had worked together on their previous film, the World War II drama *Halls of Montezuma* (1951). 'I suppose the idea of making [*Kangaroo*] originated

Fig. 1.1 Producer Robert Bassler (*left*) and director Lewis Milestone

in the Fox sales department,' Milestone said, because 'they'd accumulated a lot of money in Australia, and I suppose the only way they could move the money was to reinvest it there.'[14]

Milestone arrived in Sydney, New South Wales, on 18 August 1950.[15] 'When you sign a contract at 20th [Century Fox], they hand you a passport along with it,'[16] he joked. As luck would have it, Milestone had wanted to go to Australia in 1913 but didn't have enough money for the fare from Germany, where he was studying engineering, so he sailed to America instead because it was cheaper.[17] Other key members of *Kangaroo*'s Hollywood production team included associate producer Robert Snody (1898–1982), best known for *Green Grass of Wyoming*, who described himself as 'the man with the "headache job."'[18] Screenwriter Harry Kleiner (1916–2007), best known for the romantic musical *Carmen Jones* (1954) and the action thriller *Bullitt* (1968). The cinematographer Charles G. Clarke (1899–1983), best known for the Christmas classic *Miracle on 34th Street* (1947), *Green Grass of Wyoming*, for which he won an Academy Award, and the fantasy musical *Carousel* (1956). And last but not least, the three-time Academy Award-nominated art director Mark-Lee Kirk (1895–1969), best known for the light comedies *My Favourite Wife* (1940) and *George Washington Slept Here* (1942), and the World War II home-front drama *Since You Went Away* (1944). With so much experience and talent behind-the-scenes, and money no object, many people predicted that *Kangaroo* would put an end to Australian films characterised by 'slovenly directing, poor casting, a weakness for hayseed themes, and miserly budgets.'[19] Of course, it didn't.

Significantly, *Kangaroo* was Australia's first Technicolor film. Since it was set in and around Port Augusta (Aboriginal name Kurdnatta, meaning "place of drifting sand"), located on the east coast of the Spencer Gulf and 310 kilometres north of Adelaide, the capital of South Australia, 'where the desert meets the sea,' many moviegoers were excited by the prospect of seeing the Outback in all its Technicolor glory.[20] But being the first meant the producers had to deal with some tricky logistical problems. They had to import all of the specialist film equipment from Hollywood. 'Three Technicolor cameras, with special lighting, and the equipment necessary for Technicolor, are arriving from America shortly,'[21] *The Daily Telegraph* said. Then the Australian crew had to learn how to use the new gear, undergoing training at Ealing Studios in Sydney 'to operate the arc lights and sound apparatus and familiarise themselves with the grip equipment.'[22] Also, since there were no Technicolor laboratories in Australia, the exposed film had to be flown to America for processing, which caused delays of two to three months between shooting the scenes and viewing them. Indeed, "the tyranny of distance" in general made the Americans feel like they were embarking on 'an expedition, [...] a voyage of exploration to a never-never land which, for all they knew, was deprived of fried chicken Maryland, chocolate malted, and other benefits of the Californian littoral.'[23]

THE SCRIPT

Kangaroo began as a story by the American screenwriter Martin Berkeley (1904–1979), best known for *Green Grass of Wyoming*. In April 1949, Robert Bassler gave the American screenwriter Norman Reilly Raine (1894–1971), best known for *The Adventures of Robin Hood* (1938), the job of turning Berkeley's story into a script.[24] Also, Henry Gris of *The Sunday Herald* reported: 'Script writers at the Fox Studios are frantically reading Australian novels to get background for a film courageously called *The Australian Story*.'[25] Sufficient progress had been made by December 1949 for Robert Snody and Mark-Lee Kirk to visit Sydney to look for film locations.[26] But in 1950 Raine was replaced by Harry Kleiner, who arrived in Sydney on 28 August 1950.[27] He had a Master of Fine Arts degree from the Yale Drama School and did not fit 'the popular conception of a Hollywood writer as a cigarette smoking, liquor drinking high-pressure worker with no culture,'[28] *The Sydney Jewish News* said. Once in Australia, Kleiner quickly realised that the script as it stood was a dud and had to be rewritten. As *Smith's Weekly* explained:

> Australian authors working in the United States appear to have led Hollywood up the garden path with exciting tales about Australia. At present four American writers, assisted by an Australian, are working on the script [...] to eliminate inaccuracies. The first working script for *Kangaroo* should be ready within a week. It will be somewhat different from the original story. Authors of the first script let their heads go in a big way. They described kangaroos as big and ferocious that in dry weather they stormed bush homesteads in thousands and carried off the children [...] A hasty revision of the story is now being made to eliminate the "too fierce" kangaroos and other inaccuracies.[29]

Lewis Milestone also realised the *Kangaroo* script was no good and sought help from the Sydney Journalists' Club. 'I'm sorry the story's so bad,' he told them, so they 'promised to do whatever they could.'[30] On 29 September 1950, Milestone, Kleiner, Robert Snody, and Sydney Albright (1908–1983), the head of 20th Century Fox in Australia, had lunch at Prince's restaurant in Sydney with the prolific Australian writer Frank Clune (1893–1971) to discuss whether he could 'do some background research for the film.'[31] Milestone also visited the Australian pressman Brian Penton (1904–1951), seriously ill with kidney failure in St Luke's Hospital, 'who picked up two books from his night table and [...] said: "Please take these as a gift. Between their covers you'll find everything *I* thought worthwhile saying about Australia. You may use any part or both of them in their entirety as you see fit—it's up to you."'[32] The two books by Penton were *Landtakers: The Story of an Epoch* (1934) and *Inheritors: A Novel* (1936). Milestone liked them and 'tried to persuade the studio by long-distance telephone to scrap the damned scenario they'd sent me out with, which was a joke and substitute the Penton books.'[33] But to no avail. So, 'I fell back to my second-line trenches and resolved to narrow down the human story to the minimum and concentrate on the animals' plight during the drought,' he said. 'That way we came out of the venture with *something*, whereas otherwise, we'd have had nothing.'[34] Penton was the editor of *The Daily Telegraph*, and his mistress, the Sydney journalist Zelie McLeod (d.1993), interviewed Milestone for the newspaper. 'When we started to talk about Australia, [he] interviewed *us*,' she said. 'He wanted to know all kinds of things about this country, and he's looking for a technical adviser to make sure the conditions he shows in his film are exactly the conditions and atmosphere of Australia at the turn of the century, the period in which the film is set. [...] When we asked how he came to be making a film about Australia from a script written by an American who had never been to Australia, Milestone grinned and said: "Motion pictures and common sense are miles apart."'[35]

Milestone and Kleiner rewrote the script together (although Kleiner was sidelined for ten days with appendicitis[36]). They tried to heed the information they had received from distinguished Australian experts like the anthropologist Charles P. Mountford (1890–1976)[37] and the veterinary pathologist Harold A. Woodruff (1877–1966),[38] besides including as much local colour as possible. In the end, all that remained of Martin Berkley's story was 'a thin melodramatic plot, the basic idea,'[39] David

Bongard of *The Daily News* said. Everyone was initially coy about disclosing the story. 'You can say it is a story about a man in conflict with his conscience,' Kleiner said. 'The people of the cattle country at the turn-of-the-century provide the background.'[40] While Milestone and Kleiner were rewriting the new script, Mark-Lee Kirk and Charles G. Clarke explored Sydney and outback South Australia for film locations.[41] As soon as David F. Zanuck and Robert Bassler approved the changes to *Kangaroo*, Robert Snody gave the word for filming to start.[42]

But not everyone was happy with the new script, especially the star of *Kangaroo*, the Irish actress Maureen O'Hara (1920–2015), best known for the nostalgic dramas, *How Green Was My Valley* (1941) and *Miracle on 34th Street* (filmed by Clarke). 'I was heartbroken when I was given the revised shooting script in Sydney and saw how it had been ruined,' she said. 'Lewis Milestone had rewritten Martin Berkley's story and made it about a man and his conscience struggling with the question, "Are you a sinner if you only think about sinning, or do you actually have to commit sin to be guilty?" It was the worst piece of rubbish I had ever read. He had destroyed a good, straightforward Western.'[43] O'Hara disliked it so much that she tried to get out of doing the film but was told: 'I would be creating a huge political incident if I walked off the picture. I had no choice but to do it or be in serious trouble.'[44]

While he was much more positive than O'Hara, Snody also believed the film was no longer a Western. 'He emphasises that *Kangaroo* is not a Western,' J. Griffen-Foley of *The Film Weekly* said. 'Though there is to be action in it, it is not predominantly an action picture,'[45] Snody awkwardly told him. I believe Snody was correct to say that *Kangaroo* was not an action movie but wrong to say that it was not a Western. Perhaps a better description of it is "a scenic Western," which was what I believe the director, the screenwriter, and the cinematographer wanted to make—and in the end succeeded. For example, Clarke said he filmed it using 'a straightforward documentary style. My aim was to present the natural settings as realistically as possible [while recreating] those specially staged without using "arty" embellishments.'[46] But irrespective of what type of Western it was, making *Kangaroo* in 1950 in Australia made sense economically, as I explained earlier, and dramatically: Westerns were hugely popular, and the Australian Outback was as close to the American Wild West in spirit as you could get.

The Stars

Casting *Kangaroo*'s leading female role of Del McGuire, the faithful daughter of a drunken cattle station owner, was complicated like everything else. Robert Bassler first offered the part to the American actress Jean Peters (1926–2000).[47] Then to the English actress Jean Simmons (1929–2010), but her studio boss, J. Arthur Rank (1888–1972), refused to loan her to 20th Century Fox.[48] Then to the English actress Dawn Addams (1930-1985).[49] Then to the Irish actress Constance Smith (1929–2003),[50] who was Daryl F. Zanuck's mistress. But even that did not win her the role because Maureen O'Hara persuaded him to do a straight swap: She would replace Smith in *Kangaroo* and Smith would replace her in the noir mystery *The 13th Letter* (1951). O'Hara told him she did not like psychological roles, preferring to play 'the heroine [in *Kangaroo*, who] goes around lashing at up-to-no-good males with a bullwhip [because] Maureen wouldn't consider it a full day's work if she didn't make her leading man holler "Ouch,"' [51] the Hollywood reporter Erskine Johnson said. But according to another Hollywood reporter, Lon Jones, the swap was made because 'the studio felt that the picture needed a name player, as well as additional glamour, to sell [*Kangaroo*] to the American public.'[52]

O'Hara arrived in Sydney on 25 November 1950. She was met at the airport by 500 fans and an Irish Pipe Band. 'There's something about the Irish that makes them feel akin the world over,' she told Blake Brownrigg of *The News*. 'And their welcome did my Irish heart good.'[53] Although, in *'Tis Herself: An Autobiography* (2004), O'Hara had second thoughts: 'Every time I left my hotel and went anywhere, a bagpipe band followed me. It was lovely, but a bit too much.'[54] O'Hara's second husband Will Price (1913–1963, m.1941–1953) and their six-year-old daughter Bronwyn (1944–2016) stayed behind in Hollywood. O'Hara had planned to divorce Price before going to Australia, but John Ford (1894–1973), who had directed her in *How Green Is My Valley*, and his wife Mary (1896–1979, m.1920) talked her out of it.[55]

Casting the film's leading male role of Richard Connor, a crook with a conscience, was also very involved. Robert Bassler initially offered it to Tyrone Power (1914–1958), best known for playing swashbuckling characters like Zorro in *The Mark of Zorro* (1940). 'It might be a good deal,' he said. 'I've never been to Australia.'[56] Bassler remained hopeful that Power would accept the role, only ruling him out when they cast him as

Mister Roberts in the London production of the eponymous play (19 July 1950 to 20 January 1951).[57] Other actors in the mix to play Connor were Garry Cooper (1901–1961),[58] Clark Gable (1901–1960),[59] Cary Grant (1904–1986),[60] Alan Ladd (1913–1964),[61] William Lundigan (1914–1975),[62] Hugh Marlowe (1911–1982),[63] and Gregory Peck (1916–2003).[64] Bassler finally chose the English actor Peter Lawford (1923–1984), who Metro-Goldwyn-Mayer loaned to 20th Century Fox. While he was very popular—best known for playing opposite June Allison (1917–2006) in the musical *Good News* (1947)—he was not in the same league as many of the other actors mentioned. Lawford told the *Honolulu Star-Bulletin* on route to Australia that he was pleased to play Connor because it was his first chance to be a tough guy.[65]

Lawford arrived in Sydney on 2 November 1950. At the airport, the 27-year-old, six-foot-tall actor, 'one of the most promising and debonair of the new young Hollywood film star bachelors,'[66] was cheered and mobbed by 200 "bobby-soxers." Some were unsure about his long hair, moustache, and sideburns, which he had grown to play Richard Connor. '"He's got a beard, but I'd love him anyway," cried one excited girl after nearly falling over the railing of the visitors' enclosure. […] "Why doesn't he tear off that ziff," said another.'[67] Lawford's sex appeal was such that his lawyer, Mark Stevens, travelled with him 'to prevent him falling victim to designing females,'[68] William Latimer of *The Sydney Morning Herald* said.

The American actor Richard Boone (1917–1981) played John W. Gamble, Connor's partner-in-crime (Fig. 1.2). ("Gamble by name and gamble by nature," I guess.) Boone and Lawford travelled from Honolulu to Sydney together on the same flight. *Truth* thought they must have had energy-to-burn to spend their first night in town nightclubbing.[69] Lewis Milestone, his wife Kendall Lee (1903–1978, m.1926–1978), and her travelling companion Claire McAloon (1921–2017) accompanied the actors. Boone and McAloon fell in love in Australia and married on 27 April 1951, shortly after returning to America. He had made his film debut in the *Halls of Montezuma* and described himself as 'a New York stage actor […] learning film work from Mr. Lewis Milestone, who is a magnificent teacher.'[70] Boone is best known for playing Paladin, the debonair hired gun in the hit American Western TV series, *Have Gun Will Travel* (1957–1963). Two episodes, 'Girl from Piccadilly' (1958) and 'Hey Boy's Revenge' (1958), were directed by Milestone. Interestingly, he believed that Boone had modelled Paladin on Gamble.[71]

Fig. 1.2 Richard Boone as John W. Gamble (*left*) and Peter Lawford as Richard Connor

Before going to Australia, O'Hara, Lawford, and Boone did 'a special Australian "indoctrination" course at 20th Century-Fox,' *The Sydney Morning Herald* said. 'The studio has established a special Australian library for them. [One book O'Hara read was *Paving the Way: A Romance of the Australian Bush* (1893) by Simpson Newland (1835–1925).[72]] All three stars have seen *The Overlanders* [(1949)] and Australian documentary films. Lawford and Boone, already wearing long hair and side-whiskers in the fashion of the 1880s [sic], have been taking lessons in cracking the stockwhip. [… And] O'Hara has been learning how to ride side saddle in skirts.'[73]

The Scottish actor Finlay Currie (1878–1968) played Del McGuire's father, Michael. He had not long finished playing St Peter in *Quo Vadis* (1951) in Rome when he was 'called urgently by the […] production team here.' As a result, Currie 'gave up what would have been one of the big events of his life—the command performance of *Mudlark* [(1950)], a 20th [Century] Fox story of Queen Victoria,'[74] in which he played John Brown. Currie arrived in Australia on 7 November 1950. He had worked on stage in Australia with his wife, the American actress Maude Courtney (1884–1959), from 1911 to 1913 and 1917 to 1926. They were "patter artists," and their act was called "Maude Courtney and Mr. C." 'I played the piano while my wife sang,'[75] Currie said. 'We played all the capital cities and the backblocks too. In the backblocks, I often shared a dressing-room with a troupe of performing seals, which were travelling with our company.'[76] While making *Kangaroo*, Currie sometimes met people he had known previously and also pointed out changes since his last visit. 'Where's the old steam tram to Glenelg that used to ring a bell as soon as I started a gag?'[77] he joked when he was back in Adelaide, South Australia, in 1950.

Currie and O'Hara were nearly blacklisted in Australia because they were slow to join the Australian actors' trade union, Actors' Equity. 'If Miss O'Hara and Mr. Currie have not joined by the time they arrive, my members will be directed not to work with them,' the secretary of the union Hal Alexander (1902–1990) said. 'Miss O'Hara is reported to be getting $2000 a week, yet she refuses to pay £5 for a year's subscription.'[78] By the time the cast flew to Port Augusta to start filming, both Currie and O'Hara had joined. 'Mr. Currie said he had never refused to join this organisation but left arrangements as specified in his contract to 20th Century Fox,'[79] *The Advertiser* said.

Kangaroo was the first time O'Hara, Lawford, Boone, and Currie had worked together. Australia was a melting pot at the turn of the nineteenth century when the film was set (not the 1880s as first planned), so having an Irishwoman, an Englishman, an American, and a Scotsman in the cast did not appear—or sound—out of place. (On the other hand, when the American actor Ernest Borgnine (1917–2012) played the Australian canecutter "Roo" in *Summer of the Seventeenth Doll* (1959), set in Australia in the 1950s, his thick American accent upset both critics and moviegoers alike.) Lawford and Boone got on well together, and O'Hara and Currie got on well together. However, O'Hara strongly disliked Lawford and Boone, claiming they were rude and disrespectful to everyone. She also said that journalists had tailed them to 'a brothel full of beautiful boys' in Sydney, which 20th Century Fox managed to hush up only after she made a secret plea to the press:

> Listen, this is the first Hollywood movie ever to be made in Australia. It is very important. If you break this story, you're not just going to hurt Peter Lawford and Richard Boone, you're going to hurt me, the whole cast and crew, your own county, and the people of Australia, because the studio will shut down this picture. Australia will suffer much more than those two will.[80]

Australia was a rather glum and dowdy place after World War II and desperately in need of some glamour. Consequently, people treated the Hollywood performers like "royalty." They were in demand everywhere they went, especially O'Hara. In Sydney, for example, she did several press conferences, radio interviews, and photoshoots. She went to morning mass with Currie at St Mary's Cathedral (they were both devout Catholics). She attended a charity auction at the Celebrity Club, visited Taronga Park Zoo, and went to a press function at the Hotel Australia. She was guest-of-honour at a film industry dinner at Gleneagles restaurant and given a civic reception by the Lord Mayor of Sydney, Ernest O'Dea (1889–1976), at the Town Hall, attended by 300 people.[81] When the film stars spent 24 hours in Adelaide, the reaction was similar. They went to a garden party at Government House, a reception at the South Australian Hotel, a civic reception at Adelaide Town Hall, and a luncheon at Parliament House. O'Hara's hotel room was full of fruit and flowers given to her by fans.[82] 'Many of the flower gifts we sent to the Children's Hospital because we were flying on to our northern location so soon,' she said. 'But we did bring along most of the fruit because we didn't know how supplies would be. And I should mention the ribbons off the bouquets. I kept them all, both in Sydney and Adelaide. I use them for hair ribbons.'[83]

'We want Australians for featured roles and bit roles and extra parts,'[84] Robert Snody diplomatically announced. There were only three featured roles in *Kangaroo*. The first went to the Australian actor Chips Rafferty (1909–1971), who played Trooper "Len" Leonard, the local policeman. Rafferty was the go-to "styge Orstrylian"[85] (i.e., stage Australian), best known for *Bitter Springs* (1950) and *The Overlanders* (which O'Hara, Lawford, and Boone had watched in Hollywood, as mentioned). Lewis Milestone thought both films were fine, *The Quorn Mercury* said. 'He found them interesting, fresh, forceful.'[86] The second role went to the Australian actor Charles Tingwell (1923–2009), who played Matt, one of the McGuires' stockmen. Like Rafferty, he was also in *Bitter Springs*. Richard Boone was so impressed with Tingwell's acting that 'he contacted his agent in America about [his] possibilities.' As a result, in 1952, Tingwell made 'a rush trip to Hollywood for a film role.'[87] The third role went to the Australian actress Letty Craydon (1899–1965), who played the McGuires' housekeeper Kathleen. 'Mr. Milestone chose me for the part after seeing me in [the Charlotte Hastings play] *Bonaventure*, in which I played Sister Josephine, one of the nuns,' she told *The Daily Telegraph*. 'I am very proud and excited. It will be a wonderful break for me and of tremendous educational value. One must learn something working under a director of Milestone's calibre.'[88] 20th Century Fox opened a casting office in Sydney to select 200 people for the bit roles and extra parts needed for the city scenes filmed there. Also, hundreds of people wanting similar jobs in Port Augusta wrote to the manager of 20th Century Fox in South Australia, Mervyn Pinchbeck (1916–1983).[89]

The film's four international stars had Australian stunt doubles, especially as riding a horse could be dangerous and they were not very good at it. As mentioned, Maureen O'Hara learned how to ride side-saddle in Hollywood, although she did not have to do it in the film (Fig. 1.3). Eighteen-year-old Mary Seipelt of Sevenhill, South Australia, was her stunt double,[90] before she fell ill and was replaced by 22-year-old Nell McKay of Wilmington, South Australia.[91] Both women had started riding as children and were expert horsewomen. Peter Lawford claimed he could stay on a horse 'with the help of a little glue.' The horse he rode in *Kangaroo* was called Lawrie,[92] and his stunt double was Noel Johnston of Sydney, before he had to return home due to the sudden death of his brother and was replaced by 19-year-old Ian Jones (1931–2018) of Melbourne,[93] who went on to become a successful TV writer and producer. Richard Boone knew about horses—racehorses! 'Dick Boone's lament is that he still hasn't been to a race meeting in Australia, but he's

Fig. 1.3   Maureen O'Hara as Del McGuire on her horse

still hoping,' Blake Brownrigg said. 'He also has faith that the luck which stood to him when he backed Comic Court in the Melbourne Cup is still about the place.'[94] (In *Wild Turkey* by Max Brown, one character reads that 'two Adelaide punters had won a small fortune on Comic Court.'[95]) The horse Boone rode was called Pancho, and his stunt double was Doug Ramsay.[96] Seventy-two-year-old Finlay Currie had two nasty falls riding his horse, Robbie.[97] So, they strapped his saddle to a rig at the front of a truck and filmed him just from the waist up,[98] said Dudley Kemp (1924–2016) of Gawler, South Australia, one of the stockmen who looked after the cattle and horses used in *Kangaroo*. The former Australian heavyweight champion Jack O'Malley (1931–1932) was Currie's stunt double. He wore a wig and false nose to look more like the actor.[99]

THE STORY

Del McGuire (Maureen O'Hara) rides into town to ask her former sweetheart, Trooper Len (Chips Rafferty), about her father, Michael McGuire (Finlay Currie). She has not heard from him since he went to Sydney to get a loan to save his drought-stricken cattle station. Cut to Sydney. Michael is drunk because the bank turned him down (Fig. 1.4). He checks into a cheap dormitory-style dosshouse, suddenly feeling sorry for

Fig. 1.4 Finlay Currie as Michael McGuire

abandoning his son Dennis years ago. He gets into a fight with Burke (John Fegan), a dosshouse resident, prompting Richard Connor (Peter Lawford), another resident, to intervene on his behalf. Michael then gets the idea that Connor is Dennis.

Connor heads to the city and meets John W. Gamble (Richard Boone) leaving a two-up game. He tries to rob him, but since he lost everything, they join forces to rob Fenner (Ron Whelan), the operator of the two-up game, who Gamble shoots and kills. Now on the run, they call by the dosshouse to get Connor's swag. Michael chases them into the street, still believing Connor is Dennis, and falls down a flight of steps. While knocked out, they search his pockets and discover he owns a cattle station.

A crowd of several hundred people watched the scene being filmed at Miller's Point near the southern end of the Sydney Harbour Bridge at dusk on 11 November 1950. 'The spot was covered with arc lights, crisscrossed with electricity hose lines, and dotted with vehicles containing all the elaborate equipment needed for an important movie,'[100] *The Mail* said. They filmed Lawford and Boone running down the steps connecting Hickson Street and Windmill Street, closely followed by Currie, who falls down the last five steps, although it was his stunt double, Jack O'Malley, who took the tumble. His performance was perfect in rehearsal, but they did not film it. 'After ten minutes, the cameras whirred, and he did it again,' *The Sydney Morning Herald* said. 'His timing was wrong. The third time his wig fell off, and he lost his footing. He was shaken and bruised, but he dusted his suit and tried again. Again, he was too slow. But the next time, the director, Lewis Milestone, was satisfied, and O'Malley was out of the limelight.'[101]

Connor and Gamble discover that Michael is returning home by boat the next day, so they take him aboard and secure two berths for themselves. After Michael has sobered up, Connor and Gamble say they are returning to collect the 500 cattle he sold them for £500, which Michael believes but cannot remember. They plan to cash-in after convincing him that Connor is Dennis.

They filmed the scene onboard the Moonta (1931) on 31 January 1930 to avoid an overtime ban by Waterside Workers in early February. Seventy-three of *Kangaroo*'s cast and crew boarded the ship at 5:00 a.m. in Port Augusta. Shooting started at 6:00 a.m., shortly after it set sail, and ended at 10:00 a.m. The 130 passengers crowded the promenade deck to watch Lawford, Boone, Currie, and the extras in action. During breaks in filming, they took photographs of the stars and got their autographs. The Moonta arrived in Whyalla, South Australia, at noon—twice the time it usually took to make the journey.[102]

When they arrive, Del is upset with her father for selling them the cattle since there is no guarantee they will survive the drought. Having now found his "son," Michael stops drinking and tries even harder to save their cattle station. Trooper Len captures Matt (Charles Tingwell), an unemployed stockman, slaughtering one of their cows. Del pities him, however, and gives him a job. Then everyone helps to roundup the cattle on the McGuires' station.

Connor and Gamble suspect that Matt is a police informer, so when he rides ahead to make camp, Gamble follows him to keep watch. But bull ants bite his horse, causing it to bolt, throwing him to the ground and knocking him out. While lying unconscious, a tiger snake bites him on the leg. When Matt arrives, he kills the snake and, while attending to Gamble, discovers a scar on his ankle from leg irons. Connor finally arrives and accuses Matt of being "a copper's nark." When he denies it, Connor asks him to give Gamble another chance by keeping his criminal past a secret.

Thirteen-year-old Wendy Schneider of Burnside, South Australia, suggested the bull ants to Harry Kleiner. 'Discussion arose on what would be the best way, for a film effect, to make a horse jump and get excited when ambling through the bush [as they] didn't just want to flap something at it.'[103] Wendy's father, Dr. Michael Schneider, owned a private zoo consisting of emus, kangaroos, and koalas, and was giving the filmmakers advice about native fauna.

It was 120 degrees Fahrenheit the day they filmed the tiger snake. 'But the snake made no move—it had passed out in the heat,' *The Valley Times* said. 'Shooting was held up while propman, George Westenhiser [(1905–1973)], revived it with iced water and cooled the surrounding ground.'[104]

In charge of filming the cattle roundup was *Kangaroo*'s assistant director, Nate Watt (1889–1968), who worked on 16 films directed by Lewis Milestone between 1927 and 1959, including *Two Arabian Knights*, *All Quiet on the Western Front*, and *Pork Chop Hill* (1959). Watt also directed seven Hopalong Cassidy films between 1936 and 1939, such as *Hopalong Cassidy Returns* (1936), *Borderland* (1937), and *Law of the Pampas* (1939). According to stockman Dudley Kemp, Watt always wanted things done 'damn fast.'[105] Many locals had a pleasant day sitting outside and watching them film the roundup:

Many Port Augusta people had their first view of the *Kangaroo* production unit in action on Friday and Saturday last. The unit was shooting scenes of cattle crossing the Sandy Creek, about four miles from the town on the Whyalla road. Nine hundred cattle, a score of stockmen, and actors, including the stars, took part. Such scenes had previously been shot well off the public highways, on private ground. During Friday, scores of cars pulled up at the crossing, and hundreds of people, including many school children on holidays, sat in the shade under the Whyalla pipeline watching the proceedings. Some people made the trip from town in taxis with cut lunches and thermos flasks and spent the day enjoying the acting. Almost every child had an autograph book, and the cast, including Maureen O'Hara, Peter Lawford, Richard Boone, and Finlay Currie were kept busy in off moments.[106]

A bushfire comes from nowhere, causing wild kangaroos to hop frantically in all directions and the cattle to stampede. The scene's only purpose was to introduce some dramatic footage of kangaroos and cattle into the film. 'Australians may smile, […] but they forget that just as Australian audiences think Red Indians and gangsters career down every American street, our American audiences expect to find kangaroos in any film of Australia. So we have to show them kangaroos and cattle,'[107] Charles G. Clarke said.

At night in camp, Del and Connor go into the bush together. They nearly kiss, but Michael interrupts them, fearing they are siblings. The next day, the thirsty cattle stop at a water trough on the McGuires' station. At the same time, a thirsty tribe of Aboriginals also approach it (Fig. 1.5). An Aboriginal elder asks Michael if they can have a drink in return for performing a corroboree to make it rain. (More about it later.) Cut to the homestead. Michael, Del, Connor, and Gamble watch the corroboree while sitting on the verandah drinking tea. But instead of a rainstorm, there is a dust storm, which threatens to blow down the McGuires' windmill. Connor and Gamble toss a coin to see which one will stop it from blowing to pieces. Gamble "loses," but when he is knocked unconscious by a swinging chain, Connor bravely rescues him and fixes the windmill. Del hugs them both, but Connor more, prompting Michael to tell her that Connor is her brother. Then Connor confesses to tricking Michael before riding off with Gamble.

The police catch up to Connor and Gamble and threaten to arrest them for robbing and killing Fenner. Gamble aims his gun at Trooper Len, but Connor knocks it to the ground with his stockwhip. Then they fight each

Fig. 1.5 The thirsty Aboriginals meet the McGuires with their thirsty cattle at a water trough

other with stockwhips. Gamble eventually gets the upper hand, grabs his gun, and aims it at Connor, but Len kills him before he can shoot. Then it starts to rain. Cut to the McGuires' homestead. Connor returns a prisoner and reconciles with Del. Michael says Len will go easy on Connor in court. Cut to the town. Everyone is raucously celebrating the end of the drought. THE END.

Connor and Gamble's "duel" with stockwhips was a novel twist on the usual Western fistfight or gunfight. As a result, *Kangaroo* was called *The Law and the Whip* in some foreign counties, such as *Loven og Pisken* in Denmark and *La Ley del Latigo* in Mexico. For the final scene in the rain, the filmmakers covered the bitumen road between the Western Hotel and the Augusta Hotel in Port Augusta with sand. Ten-year-old Steve McKitterick, one of the extras, earned £5 for wrestling in the mud with two other boys.[108]

1 *KANGAROO: THE AUSTRALIAN STORY* 19

Fig. 1.6 John Endean's sketch of Connor and Gamble searching Michael McGuire

Lewis Milestone was an early pioneer of using storyboards for live-action films. He insisted on having visuals for every scene as nobody would erect a house, build a ship, or construct a bridge without committing detailed plans to paper first,[109] *The Film Weekly* said. Milestone hired John Endean, a 20-year-old Australian illustrator, to sketch the *Kangaroo* script scene-by-scene and provide him with a quick visual preview of the action. 'Working at breakneck speed doing two-minute sketches is exciting,' Endean told Rita Dunstan of *The Argus*. 'All the time you're working, you know the director is waiting for results so that he can see just how the scene will look before he orders his crew to work'[110] (Fig. 1.6).

WOOLUNDUNGA

Producer Robert Bassler originally wanted to make *Kangaroo* in rural New South Wales (NSW). However, 'his location expert reported that the NSW sites looked no different from places in Southern Arizona and California and that they would mean nothing to American audiences.'[111] Furthermore, as torrential rain had fallen from Central Australia to the eastern coastline and the film was going to depict a severe drought, they had no choice but to look elsewhere.[112] Bassler finally settled on the cattle country around Port Augusta in South Australia, which was still having a dry spell, and which everyone agreed would provide a spectacular backdrop for the first Technicolour movie made in Australia.[113]

The site for filming was Woolundunga Station, a 7000-acre "ranch" 15 miles east of Port Augusta, which belonged to Mrs. E.J. Farrell.[114] 'Weeks before work began—and months before there was an American accent in sight—the sightseers started trekking out to Woolundunga just to look at the place,' Mary Armitage of *Film Weekly* said. 'Mrs. Farrell told me she had to shoo them off the sheep yards so that she could get along with sheep drafting.'[115] Every Sunday, from 8:00 a.m. onwards, people would drive there, park their cars on the property, and stay until dusk to see where the stars would be working.[116] The name "Woolundunga" was changed to "Rooloora" for the duration of the production because 'Americans may find difficulty with the original name of the station,'[117] the film's Australian publicity director, Hartley Stuart-Codde (1898–1971) said. But apart from perhaps suggesting the name of the film, "Rooloora" was not that much easier to say.

On 25 August 1950, a public meeting was held at the Town Hall in Port Augusta to seek the cooperation of locals to ensure the speedy erection of a homestead at Woolundunga to be used for filming both exterior and interior scenes of *Kangaroo*.[118] George Fricker, the President of the Master Builders' Association of South Australia, described the filmmakers' plans for the work, while L.W. Abernethy, the Town Clerk of Port Augusta, explained their policy to employ as many people and to buy as many things locally as possible.

Information about Australia in general—let alone traditional homesteads—was hard to find in Hollywood: 'We have very little information about Australia in America,'[119] *Kangaroo*'s American production manager Paul Wurtzel (1921–2014) said. So, instead of a typical sprawling one-storey house, the film's art director Mark-Lee Kirk designed a most uncharacteristic—possibly even Antebellum-style—two-storey house. The Australian construction crew was to follow a detailed scale model of the building made in Hollywood, *The News* said.[120] To make filming simpler, it looked like a two-storey house from the outside but had only a ground floor on the inside.[121] After the locals told them they were on the wrong track, they wisely sent a team of researchers out to examine photographs of old Australian homesteads in the NSW Archives and look at similar old buildings in other states. Henceforth, the chastened filmmakers took great pains 'to ensure that no smart Australian will be able to find fault,'[122] R.M.E. of *The Whyalla News* said.

On 28 August 1950, *Kangaroo*'s cinematographer Charles G. Clarke, Colin Hall, an Australian filmmaker who was helping to get cattle and kangaroos for the film, and Wurtzel chose the site for the homestead, about two miles off the Wilmington Road, with picturesque Mount Brown in the background. 'We have pinpointed the place, and it is a good position,'[123] they agreed. Then the Wilmington District Council obligingly built a new road to the site,[124] enabling them to clear the vegetation and begin constructing the six-room farmhouse they had finally settled on. It also had a stockyard. A 100-year-old windmill they had found in the Adelaide suburb of Glenelg.[125] A 67-year-old pump that syphoned water—albeit from a barrel buried underground.[126] A vertical-split-log-paling cookhouse with an iron roof.[127] A stable for horses, which was deliberately placed so that Port Augusta, visible in the distance, was blotted out.[128] And a garden of wilted shrubs and dead trees held erect by "invisible" wires.[129] Steve McKitterick said that 'they tied crows to the branches. They had bands around their wings, so they wouldn't hurt them.'[130] Even pot plants supplied by an Adelaide nursery were deliberately left in the sun without water so they would have a withered appearance,[131] R.M.E. said.

The filmmakers built the homestead using the same principles as a Hollywood sound stage. The heavy-duty floor, consisting of Oregon timber boards, 12 inches by 2 inches, supported on 90 concrete piers, was designed to prevent it from dipping and shaking and thus facilitating the smooth movement of the heavy and sensitive Technicolor film cameras. They purchased the 50,000 square feet of Oregon floorboards required locally from Cowell Bros' timberyard in Port Augusta.[132] As there was a shortage of building materials in Australia following World War II, the filmmakers promised to dispose of the timber in the district when filming ended.[133] It was possible to quickly remove some of the walls without affecting the stability of the homestead, enabling the cameras to move freely from room to room and work from almost any angle. Boardwalks above the ceiling-less bedrooms, parlour, and living room held the banks of powerful arc lamps needed to make the Technicolor film, which required ten times more lighting than black and white films. According to the Hollywood electrician Charles Wise (1904–1991), the homestead had 'enough lighting for a small town'[134] (Fig. 1.7).

Fig. 1.7 The homestead built for *Kangaroo* on Woolundunga Station

Led by expert Hollywood set painter Johnny Lawless, the *Kangaroo* team of painters skilfully "aged" the homestead's new weatherboard exterior and galvanised iron roof with paint. 'The paintwork round much-used door handles appears to have been worn away, rust stains the iron roof and water tanks,'[135] Blake Brownrigg said. Also, they painted one side of Mrs. Farrell's house and the domed galvanised iron cover over the Davenport Reservoir with special dull paint to prevent any reflections from being picked up by the sensitive film cameras during filming,[136] and sprayed the ground and vegetation with black paint to create the effect of darkness.[137] The filmmakers were true to their word and bought the paint locally. A newspaper ad for Colton's, a South Australian paint distributor, said they used 'hundreds of gallons of Sherwin-Williams Paint and Kem-Tone […] in both the exteriors and interiors of the "sets" for the production of the film *Kangaroo*.'[138]

They paid the same attention to detail on the interior of the homestead. For example, they used period-style flock wallpaper with a rough texture so it would not reflect light, imported specially from Hollywood.[139] They decided to source props locally instead of relying on those from Ealing Studios in Sydney and asking the public for help when they couldn't find everything. As the date for filming approached, George Westenhiser was anxious to find ten Winchester or Marlin lever-action rifles, ten Colt .44 single-action frontier-model revolvers, ten saddles with large knee and thigh pads, two Victorian-style double beds with six feet high headboards,[140] six frosted glass gas lamp shades with fluted tops,[141] and six kerosene table lamps between 24 and 30 inches high.[142] In the end, a second-hand shop in Adelaide came to their rescue, supplying them with all the furniture, bric-a-brac, art work, and fine china for the homestead.[143] Brownrigg was very impressed with the result:

> Chandeliers hang in the entrance hall and rooms, which are filled with tasselled curtains and tablecloths, heavy ornaments, kerosene lamps, and florid statuary. Attention to detail is amazing. Pick up a book anywhere, and it might be a volume of Scott's, a Bible, a faded family album in exquisitely tooled leather, or maybe a book of songs, one of which bears the stirring title, 'Mother, Can This the Glory Be?' Ancestral portraits adorn the walls, the men wearing fierce mutton-chop side whiskers, the women draped demurely over any convenient rose-covered garden wall.[144]

A gang of men working well over 40 hours per week finished the homestead in time for the start of filming on 21 December 1950.[145] Estimates of its cost ranged from £15,000[146] to £30,000.[147] To facilitate the demolition of the homestead later, they used four-inch double-headed nails, also specially imported from Hollywood, which they hammered down to the second head, so they could be removed without prising them from the wood first (Fig. 1.8). However, the Hollywood set builder in charge of construction, Walter Fitchman (1901–1988), could not convince the local carpenters to use only enough nails to keep the homestead standing. 'Our chaps wanted to make things secure and often used half a dozen nails where one would do,'[148] Lawrie Jervis of *The News* said with misplaced pride. According to Heather Summerton, who lives next to Woolundunga Station on Catninga Station, the homestead was pulled apart and turned into a shearing shed after the cast and crew left. What remains of it is now a storage shed.[149]

Fig. 1.8   A four-inch double-headed nail

Heat, Willy-Willies, and Flies

Making *Kangaroo* at the height of summer in Port Augusta, one of the hottest places in Australia, was very challenging. When asked why they had not made the film during the colder—and thus perhaps wetter—months of the year, Hartley Stuart-Codde said that would have been 'too silly for words' because it was about a drought.[150] But the extreme heat caused everyone a lot of discomfort. The day Maureen O'Hara arrived in Port Augusta it was 110 degrees Fahrenheit. 'I would ask people if it was like this all the time [...] and they would pretend to be surprised and say, "Why this is lovely. Just wait till it starts to get hot." And I believed them! I was beginning to get really panicky.'[151] The heat prompted them to install a metal swimming tank, 25 feet wide and six deep, for the *Kangaroo* cast and crew to use.[152] 'Then some idiot named it "Polio Plunge," and the inviting pool was little used thereafter,'[153] Blake Brownrigg said. (There was a worldwide polio pandemic in 1950.) The heat also caused technical problems, such as keeping the highly sensitive motion picture film cool. 'A ton of ice will be used daily by the film company to keep its Technicolor film in condition before shooting,' *The Advertiser* said. 'Stocks have to be maintained at a temperature of 50 degrees.'[154] Also, water used straight from the tap was too hot for the 900 cattle in the film to drink, so the stockmen looking after them had to cool it in tanks first.[155]

Besides the heat, the cast and crew also had to endure creepy crawlies. A swollen mosquito bite over O'Hara's right eye prevented her from filming for three days,[156] while a spider bite gave *Kangaroo*'s 27-year-old sound engineer, James Flanagan, pains in the stomach and groin and paralysed him down one side for the best part of a day.[157] But undoubtedly the biggest pest for everyone was the flies (*Musca vetustissima*). 'My complaint is that your South Australian flies stick,'[158] O'Hara told Norman Meares of *The Advertiser*. The Lord Mayor of Adelaide, Arthur Rymill (1907–1989), advised her to first let them settle—then get used to them![159] However, a fly walking across a star's face on camera caused delays and cost the studio money. Therefore, George Westenhiser had to make sure it did not happen. 'It looks like I will have to go around with a spray gun in my pocket to keep the flies off Maureen O'Hara's face,'[160] he said. He meant it because newsreel footage showed him doing exactly that (Fig. 1.9).[161] O'Hara's only protection was a handkerchief covering her face! Of course, we now know that DDT is a dangerous carcinogen. Ironically, when the filmmakers did want flies in a scene, they stubbornly refused to oblige:

1 KANGAROO: THE AUSTRALIAN STORY   25

Fig. 1.9 George Westenhiser (*right*) spraying Maureen O'Hara with DDT

'Fifty men of the 20th Century Fox unit, including director Milestone and camera and sound crews, worked for three hours yesterday morning on the set at Woolundunga Station, trying to film two of the most uncooperative actors in the world,' *The News* said.

> The actors were two house flies, and the aim was to get shots of Peter Lawford and Richard Boone betting on which would win in a race up the windowpane, and of the flies taking off before the "finishing post." [...] Property assistant Eric Wenban of Sydney caught two dozen flies by hand and put them in a bottle. Then came the job of sticking them to the window and getting them to fly off at the right moment in the right direction. This was done with the aid of honey, a piece of cotton, and DDT.[162]

Willy-willies or dust storms were another annoyance. One time a willy-willy suddenly descended on the film unit unheeded. It spooked Richard Boone's horse, causing it to madly gallop off into the distance with him hanging on grimly. It also blew Lewis Milestone's hat 100 feet into the air. Maureen O'Hara had to cling to her hat with one hand while trying to quieten her mount with the other. Script supervisor Stanley Scheuer (1900–1983) was thrown against a camera and broke his watch. But most amusingly, it blew makeup artist Jimmy Barker's false teeth into the saltbush after he had removed them due to the heat and placed them on a chair. When a second willy-willy struck a short time later, Milestone and O'Hara were ready for it, posing before the camera amidst the frenzy to show their friends in Hollywood.[163]

Fortunately, cinematographer Charles G. Clarke was able to turn the ever-present dust storms to his advantage. 'Thus, when we discovered that dust was to be with us whenever the earth's surface was touched, we deliberately made use of its pictorial aspect,' he said. 'In shooting scenes of the animal herds, we frequently chose camera angles to take advantage of the dust effects rather than for the direction of the light.'[164] But due to the dust, cameramen Scotty McEwin and Lou Konkel had to take the cameras apart at the end of each day to clean and check for scratches on the lenses. And because of the wind, much of the outdoor dialogue was inaudible and had to be dubbed in the studio later. As a result, '*Kangaroo* will carry more dubbed sound than any film the company has made before,'[165] L. McGovern of *The Sunday Herald* claimed. Thus it was very ironic that the filmmakers had to import ten tons of dust in the form of Fuller's earth because 'the genuine red stuff does not film so effectively' in close-ups of the actors.[166] It was also supposed to be gentler on their eyes and skin, although, one time, O'Hara 'still got an eyeful of grit that held up work for a couple of hours,'[167] *The News* said. The filmmakers hired two Avro-Anson aeroplane engines from Guinea Airways, so Milestone could create a dust storm at will any time. All this prompted one old timer to remark in disbelief: 'By ghost, I never reckoned I'd live to see the day they imported dust into Australia.'[168]

Terra Nullius

On 8 January 1951, a party of 80 Aboriginals—40 men, 23 women, and 17 children—arrived in Port Augusta by train from Ooldea Mission, 536 miles away on the eastern edge of the Nullarbor Plain, to appear in *Kangaroo*.[169] The filmmakers employed them rather than Aboriginals from Port Augusta because they had been in *Bitter Springs* (1950) and were already "experienced" actors. Although, it has to be said they did not treat them like movie stars. For appearing in *Kangaroo*, the Ooldea people were paid only the basic wage [eight pounds six shillings and sixpence

(£8/6/6) per week] or the equivalent amount in goods and they lived in tents on the banks of Spear Creek, 19 miles east of Port Augusta.[170] 'The tent floors were covered with straw palliasses, and clothes hung along the ridge poles,' Max Brown observed when he visited the camp.

> Under a tree, ten men were seated on the ground making woomeras and shields. They held the wood between their heels and their sharp chisels struck quick, rhythmical blows, dangerously near the flesh. [...] I passed a newly completed shower block and came on a group of women baking rabbits on a fire. Down the gorge came men carrying more rabbits and short sticks. They told me there were rabbits and mountain kangaroos—euros— up the gorge. [... In a storeroom, Brown saw] 'bundles of spears and woomeras, boxes of boomerangs, and wooden dishes the Ooldea women use for digging out rabbits and carrying water. These were for use in the film. Against the walls were bags of potatoes and onions, cases of honey, soap, tea, and other items contractors supplied to the Aborigines Protection Board, which was running the camp. [The cook, former missionary Herbert Reichenbach,] told me the aborigines had eaten three cases of oranges in their first two days in camp but liked meat best of all foods.[171]

On 16 January 1951, the producers of *Kangaroo* arranged a special screening of *Bitter Springs* at the Port Augusta Town Hall for the Ooldea people to remind them of the task ahead. 'There were loud cheers when the aborigines first appeared on the screen, but the greatest excitement was when the Ooldea aborigines—most of whom had never seen a film before—saw themselves and their friends and relatives giant-size before them,'[172] *The News* said. Also in attendance were most of the *Kangaroo* cast and crew, including those actors who had been in *Bitter Springs* as well—Chips Rafferty, Charles Tingwell, and Aboriginal elders and actors Clyde Combo, who played a stockman in *Kangaroo*, and Henry Murdoch (1920–1987), who played a tracker.

The producers of *Kangaroo* wanted all of the Aboriginal men in the film to have long hair, including Uncle Clyde and Uncle Henry. Therefore, when the Australian special effects man Roger Tierney thought their hair was too short, he warned them: 'If you boys don't grow long hair and beards more quickly, I'll glue them on.'[173] He was not joking because he had a large stock of hair for wigs, moustaches, and beards. 'To make a life-like moustache occupies two to three hours because every hair must be tied separately with a special needle onto a transparent backing which can be attached to the skin,' Tierney told Blake Brownrigg. 'Neatly pinned to a large board in his room, Tierney has the moustaches of stars, feature players, and extras with their nametags, ready for use on location,'[174] Brownrigg observed. While the third assistant director, David Moore, had to check the length of the Ooldea men's hair. 'Some wore it short. Others had knitting wool bound round their temples, so the hair came out on top like a daisy,'[175] he said. Although, if necessary, the filmmakers were willing to go well beyond just long hair to make the Ooldea men appear "savage" on the screen. When *Kangaroo*'s technical advisor, Colin Simpson (1908–1983), learned that nearly all of the Ooldea men had holes through their noses, he arranged for the chicken bones to be kept and cleaned after dinner so they could wear them the next day for their first scene.[176] Thankfully, they did not have to in the end.

On 29 January 1951, at Corraberra Station, about nine miles from Port Augusta,[177] the filmmakers shot *Kangaroo*'s most poignant scene featuring the Ooldea people. As mentioned, a mob of thirsty Aboriginals and a herd of thirsty cattle owned by the McGuires happen upon a water trough at the same time. The Aboriginals are on one side, and the McGuires and their cattle are on the other, so to speak. Even though the Aboriginals are heavily armed with spears and boomerangs, they very politely ask Michael McGuire's permission to drink from the water trough, promising in return to do a corroboree to end the drought later on at the homestead. Speaking their language (Kokatha?), Michael invites them to go ahead. The Aboriginals are then shown drinking from the water trough before the picture fades to one of the cattle drinking from the same trough. But the implication is clear: 'The Indigenous Australians are just another type of livestock that serve a specific purpose on the cattle station—in their case, making rain,'[178] said Daniel Eisenberg, a curator of photographs, film, and sound at the Australian War Memorial. How did this lamentable equivalence originate? I believe it was the racist doctrine of *terra nullius*, Latin for "nobody's land." But before I explain this further, let me describe the history of this scene from *Kangaroo*, which is perhaps even more shockingly racist since the Aboriginals were, in fact, only a poor substitute for kangaroos in the filmmakers' eyes.

Initially, the makers of *Kangaroo* imagined a terrific battle between 1000 thirst-crazed kangaroos and the McGuires and their cattle for the last remaining waterhole (Fig. 1.10).[179] 'This sequence will compare with any of the great cattle and horse stampedes filmed,' Bassler enthused. 'It will be the most unique thing ever put on the screen. It could become the most talked-about scene in the history of movies.'[180] He also believed it

1 KANGAROO: THE AUSTRALIAN STORY   29

Fig. 1.10   Poster for *Kangaroo* showing marauding kangaroos

would help to put Australia on the tourist map. 'Imagine what that's likely to do to the tourist business alone. Why, everyone will want to visit the country to see the kangaroos in their natural state.'[181] Bassler took a while to realise that rounding up 1000 kangaroos was virtually impossible. 'We've got experienced men rounding up the kangaroos, but the 'roos sure can run,'[182] he said. The filmmakers reduced their target to 300 kangaroos, which was the minimum number they thought they could get away with using trick photography.[183] They were willing to beg, borrow, or buy kangaroos for £5 per head from the public, governments, zoos, anyone—but, alas, it was still all to no avail.[184] 'The unit has had difficulty in getting sufficient kangaroos for a scene,' L. McGovern said. 'It wanted hundreds but so far has only mustered three or four.'[185]

Bassler feared that without the spectacular kangaroo scene, 'the picture will lose much of its appeal for Americans.'[186] As a result, publicity posters for *Kangaroo* dishonestly showed Richard Connor trying to protect Del McGuire from hundreds of marauding Aboriginals, cattle, and kangaroos. It does not happen in the film, although the filmmakers dearly wished it had. While two joeys hop about the McGuires' verandah at the beginning of the film and there is footage of kangaroos fleeing a bushfire, even Charles G. Clarke admitted that 'kangaroos have little to do with the story.'[187] To justify *Kangaroo*'s title, they briefly suggested that John W. Gamble was known as "The Kangaroo" but quickly dropped it.[188] After failing to get 300—let alone 1000—kangaroos, they came up with the idea of the Aboriginals and the cattle at the water trough. Shamefully, their decision to essentially replace the kangaroos with the Aboriginals was in keeping with what most white people thought in the 1950s. Until the High Court of Australia overturned *terra nullius* in 1992, according to the law, Australia was "nobody's land" before European colonisation in 1788, which meant that for a long time the status of First Nations Australians was more akin to fauna than landowners.

As mentioned, in return for letting the Aboriginals drink, they performed a rainmaking dance. The principal dancers wore tall, feathered headdresses, while lines of white bird down ran along their arms, over their chests and stomachs, and down their legs. They performed a total of five dances, in fact: (1) the Kipara or "Wild Turkey" dance, which was the source of the title of Max Brown's novel, *Wild Turkey*; (2) the Mamu or "Evil Spirits" dance; (3) the Tarrawanna (no translation) dance; (4) something they described as "a play about dance"; and (5) the rainmaking dance. According to Colin Simpson and Charles P. Mountford:

> At the beginning of the rainmaking corroboree, an old rainmaker decorated with bird down and painted designs and wearing his high headdress, is seated on the ground. He is rubbing the sacred rainmaking stone—the ringili (an engraved pearl shell)—across a flat boulder covered with blood. Seated on either side of him are three Aboriginals, similarly decorated, but wearing smaller headdresses, who chant the magical songs of the ceremony. In Aboriginal mythology, the rain-stone is a concentrated mass of the kuranita (life essence) of water and consequently rain. The fragments of the pearl shell removed by the rubbing will go into the sky and aided by the chants of the song men and later rituals will form into rain clouds. Into the scene enters a line of painted men, boomerangs in either hand, dancing sinuously behind a leader who carries a tall totemic rain-board on which is painted the symbol of the Rainbow Serpent. It is an immense varicoloured creature that lives in deep caverns under permanent waterholes and clouds and is associated with rain in rainmaking. As these men circle the rainmaker and the songsters, they raise their hands and boomerangs towards the sky. This is done to project the essence of the rain released by the rainmaker into the sky in the form of clouds. Suddenly, there appears four grotesquely decorated figures, dancing furiously to avoid the dancers who are advancing in pursuit. They are the Mamu-wati (Devil-men), who if they are not destroyed will nullify the effects of the rainmaking ceremony through evil spirits they control. Finally, the Mamu-wati are overcome and fall to the ground, and the dancers pass over them with a wild shout, throwing their boomerangs into the sky.[189]

Lewis Milestone assured the Ooldea people that no Aboriginal boys or women would ever see *Kangaroo* because only initiated Aboriginal men could witness the sacred and secret rainmaking corroboree. 'They didn't care about us,'[190] Milestone said. It was an empty promise, however, because the dancers spotted an Aboriginal woman among the onlookers, and immediately halted the corroboree. The filmmakers arranged for her to sit in a car some distance away, but when the sharp-eyed dancers noticed that she was still looking, they stopped dancing again. So, the woman was driven to Port Augusta, 13 miles away. After three days, the non-stop corroboree ended with the Ooldea people throwing their boomerangs in the air to celebrate. On 16 February 1951, the producers held a special screening of Westerns and cartoons at the Port Augusta Town Hall to thank them for their excellent work on the film,[191] and on 20 February 1951, they departed for Ooldea Mission.[192]

The Ooldea people and the cast and crew seemed to get on well despite their cultural differences and social disparities. According to Chips Rafferty, the Aboriginals quickly developed a taste for American-style hotcakes and Coca-Cola and, as a result, 'there wasn't a goanna grilling for miles round.'[193] Maureen O'Hara knew something of Aboriginal dance before coming to Australia, having read about Mosick (d.1950), the Waugaite elder and dancer described by the American modern dance expert, Ted Shawn (1891–1972), as 'the greatest natural dancer in the world.'[194] O'Hara befriended a shy three-year-old Ngalia boy and his mother, who lived 400 miles northwest of Ooldea and came to Port Augusta for *Kangaroo*. She even learned a few words of their language (Warlpiri?) and sometimes began her letters to her daughter back home with '"Nuru Tichi Chuku Chuku Nambi Bronwyn" (My Dear Little Child Bronwyn).'[195] She also thought that the Aboriginals were 'the best actors in the film.'[196] Peter Lawford admired the Aboriginals' expert throwing skills, and one of the best exponents taught him how to throw a boomerang.[197] Lewis Milestone was full of praise for the Aboriginals' dancing abilities, which had inspired half the crew to try out the steps and rhythms of the corroborees for themselves.[198] Reflecting on early Australian Westerns made decades before *Kangaroo*, the veteran Sydney journalist and screenwriter Gayne Dexter (1890–1966) said: 'Forty years ago, cowboys rode Bondi sandhills; La Perouse aborigines wore redskins' feathers, wielded tomahawks and spears. They were acting in some of our early Australian productions of American Westerns costing just £75. Now, reversing history, here's an Australian Western produced by Americans for £750,000 or thereabouts.'[199]

Zanuckville

The shortage of housing in Australia following World War II was so severe it jeopardised the making of *Kangaroo*, as there was nowhere to accommodate the cast and crew. Fortunately, the Premier of South Australia, Thomas Playford (1896–1981), stepped in to assist, believing that by making the film off the beaten track in remote Port Augusta, the whole of the state would benefit. 'It will convey […] an idea of the scenery to be found in South Australia and will be a wonderful advertisement for our State overseas,'[200] he said. Without Playford's help, 'the film simply could not have been made,' Charles G. Clarke declared. 'It so happened that housing facilities were soon to be built for an electric power project near Port Augusta. The [Premier] purposely moved this building program ahead so that it would become available for our use. He also made it possible for us to obtain the construction materials necessary for our sets.'[201]

The South Australian government completed the 24 houses for the film stars, technicians, cooks, maids, carpenters, and so on in record time (Fig. 1.11).[202] It helped that they were mass-produced and that the trade unions allowed people to work on them six days a week.[203] Thus 'in less than a month, a big temporary housing area has grown like a mushroom

Fig. 1.11 Zanuckville, Port Augusta, South Australia (c.1950)

just out of the township,'²⁰⁴ *The News* reported. The new suburb was named "Hollywood Park" by the locals, but the cast and crew knew which side their bread was buttered, quickly renaming it "Zanuckville" after their boss Darryl F. Zanuck. 'Many thanks for naming *Kangaroo* film city after me,' he said. 'This is indeed an unexpected honour.'²⁰⁵ When they had finished building it, Playford officially handed the keys over to Robert Snody on behalf of 20th Century Fox. 'With the Stars and Stripes and the Australian flag fluttering in the hot north wind,' he declared: '"We hope the members of the company will be very happy here and we hope the conditions will be so congenial that a really great film will be made." [He] added that the people of Port Augusta and the State Government would do anything possible to ensure the success of the film.'²⁰⁶ Peter Lawford, Finlay Currie, Richard Boone, Chips Rafferty, and Charles Tingwell also spoke at the ceremony.²⁰⁷ Each house had 'three bedrooms, a bathroom containing two showers, a laundry, a septic tank, and the latest kerosene burners for heating water.'²⁰⁸ Being only 'of the standard emergency type,'²⁰⁹ they were very modest compared to Hollywood houses. Although, to compensate for the lack of luxury, the *Kangaroo* cast and crew received clean bed linen, fresh fruit, and plenty of iced water in their rooms every day.²¹⁰ Currie was very happy with his house, insisting on showing Playford around and telling him: 'Isn't it just what the doctor ordered? Where would you find better?'²¹¹ The house-proud actor even grew some potplants outside his front door. '"We will be here about three months," he said. "We might as well make the place as homey as possible."'²¹² *The News* aptly described Zanuckville as a 'strange community of exotic growth, surely Australia's most unusual town.'²¹³

Maureen O'Hara patriotically named her house "Shamrock Lodge," which she had painted in green next to the front door, along with Ireland's coat-of-arms, the Harp of Erin.²¹⁴ But it was far from her stylish, two-storey, Georgian mansion in the chic Los Angeles suburb of Bel Air. Indeed, O'Hara had gone from 'a luxury Hollywood home in the film colony's most exclusive residential area to a shack in the sun-baked film camp at Zanuckville,'²¹⁵ Blake Brownrigg said.

> Her rooms are not carpeted, but covered with lino squares, the chairs being of rather stiff high-backed period design, with a lounge of the same style. On a small table in the living room were photos of her adorable little girl. A large double frame held a picture of husband, Mr. W.C. Price, and daughter, Bronwyn, taken just prior to her leaving America. [...] She also had a photo of three generations—her own mother (a fine-looking woman), herself, and

her small daughter. [...] Her hut is air conditioned and contains its own cooking hot point, electric jug, and a wood stove. Outside her door is a small rotary clothesline which is used quite often.[216]

A newspaper ad for the iconic Australian rotary clothesline, the Hills Hoist, showed O'Hara hanging up the washing at Shamrock Lodge. 'Another of Hills Hoist many satisfied customers!' the ad declared. 'Whenever she can, Maureen O'Hara attends to all the usual domestic chores. She was trained to be practical and, like many thousands of Australian housewives, selected the Hills Hoist Rotary Clothes Hoist for convenience and efficiency.'[217] I very much doubt it!

The largest and most impressive building in Zanuckville was the mess hall where the *Kangaroo* cast and crew ate together. British workers from Ealing Studios built it without blueprints,[218] no doubt relying on their memories of army mess halls during World War II. It was 22 by 80 feet[219] and built off the ground on stilts.[220] It had a Baltic pine floor, walls consisting of Masonite at the bottom and flywire at the top, and a canvas roof.[221] Next to the mess hall was the kitchen, which was 40 by 50 feet.[222] It had four oil-burning stoves, an eight-gallon deep-fryer,[223] and a cool store, ten by 12 feet.[224] Breakfast was at 7:00 a.m. and dinner at 8:00 p.m.[225] Lunch was often served in the field. 'To slake the thirst of the company on location in the heat the unit sends out huge thermos flasks of iced fruit and milk drinks,' *The News* said. 'Everyone is issued with a collapsible cup. At lunchtime, 90 men line up for heaped platefuls of crisp salads or beautifully cooked crumbed cutlets and vegetables. For sweets, fruit salad and cream are provided. All those with the company have put on weight and are brown as lifesavers.'[226]

The similarities between Zanuckville and the film colony in *Wild Turkey* by Max Brown are plain to see. It was named "Glitzburg," after Walter Z. Glitz, the head of Colossus, the Hollywood film studio making the movie *Wild Turkey*. Built by the government to house workers on a uranium lease, Glitzburg consisted of 'twenty asbestos prefabs, laid out in four rows with kitchen and large mess hall in the centre, and behind against the saltbush a garage and a power plant,' which was loaned to the film studio while they made the movie in Broken Hill, New South Wales.[227]

The mess hall was the hub of Zanuckville's social life. *Kangaroo*'s Australian publicity officer, 23-year-old Thalia Lawson, and her newlywed husband, the English businessman and socialite Bill Welch, held their wedding there on 23 December 1950. Many of the cast and crew attended: Lewis Milestone gave the bride away, his wife Kendall Lee was the matron-of-honour, and Robert Snody was the best man.[228] The next day, the

Zanuckville community celebrated Christmas Eve there. 'Tinsel and coloured lights will decorate a huge Christmas tree erected in the main mess hall at the film town of Zanuckville,' *The News* said. 'Gifts will be distributed on Christmas Eve—American style—by film stars Maureen O'Hara, Peter Lawford, Richard Boone, and other cast members.'[229] The day after, they sat down to Christmas lunch in the mess hall—chicken, ham, lobster, turkey, green peas, plum pudding, ice cream, fruit cake, mince pies, mixed nuts, and sweets were on the menu.[230] (The abundance of food was rather embarrassing given that post-war food rationing had only ended in July 1950. So, when they learned that the larder at the nearby Port Augusta Hospital was bare, they 'rushed turkeys and other Christmas fare to the hospital.'[231]) And on 31 December 1930, the cast and crew held a New Year's Eve party in the mess hall.

It was difficult for the Americans to call their families and friends in the USA—not least because there was only one telephone, located in a phone box on Zanuckville's main street.[232] Thus on 15 December 1950, they visited the radio station at Port Augusta to record Christmas messages for loved ones back home, Brownrigg said. 'The discs will be flown to the United States and broadcast on Christmas Eve.'[233] Even so, many still lined up to use Zanuckville's solitary phone box. 'That for them will be the climax of Christmas, 1950,'[234] *The News* said.

There was not much to do in Zanuckville at the end of the day. O'Hara's radiogram and records had not arrived as expected, so she could not listen to her favourite music at Shamrock Lodge.[235] On 14 January 1951, she and Currie attended a concert by the musical Hakendorf family at the Commonwealth Hotel in Port Augusta.[236] It reminded him of 'the old days before radio and cinema when you could go along to visit friends, everyone would gather around the piano, someone would bring out a violin or cello, and there would be music.'[237] They also visited the library in town since, 'in the film camp, good books are as rare as kangaroos,'[238] Norman Meares of *The Advertiser* said sarcastically. O'Hara went shopping in Port Augusta 'just like everyone else,'[239] one long-time resident recalled. She bought 'a gardener's straw hat' for herself on one occasion,[240] and a silver egg cup and spoon for her daughter Bronwyn on another.[241] O'Hara also went to special events sometimes. For example, on 24 January 1951, she attended the South Australian premiere of the film *Bagdad* (1949) at the Port Augusta Town Hall, in which she played Princess Marjan. 'It was decided that owing to Miss O'Hara being in Port Augusta playing the feminine lead in the 20th Century Fox production *Kangaroo*, to give this town the honour of showing *Bagdad* before it commences its Adelaide season,'[242] *The Transcontinental* reported.

Peter Lawford brought his custom-made 30-ounce balsawood surfboard to Australia,[243] but he could not use it in Port Augusta, so he and Richard Boone spent their spare time shooting rabbits with pea rifles they bought in town.[244] Boone certainly kept himself very busy. On 26 January 1951, he and former champion boxer Jack O'Malley, Finlay Currie's stunt double, refereed an amateur boxing contest between Whyalla and Port Augusta at the Port Augusta Town Hall.[245] Robert Snody presented the trophies to the winners.[246] Boone also drank at the Hotel Flinders in Port Augusta, where he befriended three-year-old Christopher Millane, who lived there with his grandparents. The actor gave the youngster 'a pair of highly decorated, handmade cowboy boots [and thereafter] almost any night [they] can be found in an upstairs passage [...] repelling an Apache attack,'[247] *The Mail* said. Also, as mentioned previously, Boone was dating Claire McAloon. But theirs was not the only romance to bloom Down Under—George Westenhiser met his future wife Cherry Wheatley there too.[248]

On 22 February 1951, the cast and crew of *Kangaroo* held a farewell party in the mess hall to thank the citizens of Port Augusta for their help. They gave the Mayor, Lindsay Riches (1904–1972), a copy of a newsreel showing the arrival of the stars, the official welcome, and the opening of Zanuckville. They also gave Peg Howard a cheque and a bound copy of the *Kangaroo* script for recruiting the local extras.[249] While the citizens presented O'Hara with a clock mounted in a stirrup and Boone with an Australian sheepdog named "Aussie."[250] After the dog was quarantined in the USA, he finally received it on the set of his next film, *Red Skies of Montana* (1952).[251]

On 17 March 1951, Elder Smith & Co. Ltd. auctioned hundreds of goods and chattels from Zanuckville, including buildings, kitchen appliances, motor vehicles, and even 'the bed that Maureen O'Hara slept in.'[252] Over 1000 people attended the sale. 'All goods were practically new, and bidding was keen,' *The Advertiser* said. 'Many articles brought more than the new price. Building material, piping, wire netting, troughing, and other "hard to get" articles required for pastoral holdings, were very keenly sought.'[253] They also sold the 900 cattle used in the film at the Stirling sale yards,[254] and the 19 horses at the Brooklyn Park sale yards.[255] Workers on the northern regional power station then leased the Zanuckville houses for 30 shillings per week.[256] But they considered that was too much, so the South Australian government reduced their rent by four shillings. As homes for film stars went, they were hardly luxurious.

The Critics

Predictably, kangaroos featured heavily in publicity for *Kangaroo*. In September 1951, the Australian cinema chain Hoyt's and 20th Century Fox held a beauty contest to choose "Miss *Kangaroo*," which was won by Loretta North, a 19-year-old model from Sydney. Accompanied by two ten-month-old, four feet high kangaroos named Joey and Matilda, she visited 32 cities in America and Canada to promote the film (Fig. 1.12).[257] Sadly, Matilda died from cold in New York. 'The Sydney, Australia, papers made a big fuss about it. You'd think the Americans had poisoned her or something,'[258] Miss *Kangaroo* protested, alluding to the suspicious death of the champion New Zealand-bred racehorse Phar Lap in the USA in 1932. In Washington DC, the un-housetrained Joey sat on North's lap and "ruined" her designer black silk cocktail dress. There were other bizarre publicity stunts as well. In May 1952, Edward J. Hallstrom (1886–1970), the chairman of Taronga Park Zoo in Sydney, travelled to Washington DC to present US President Harry Truman (1884–1972) with an albino kangaroo or 'a white kangaroo for the White House.'[259] In a joint statement from Australia's Acting Prime Minister, Sir Arthur

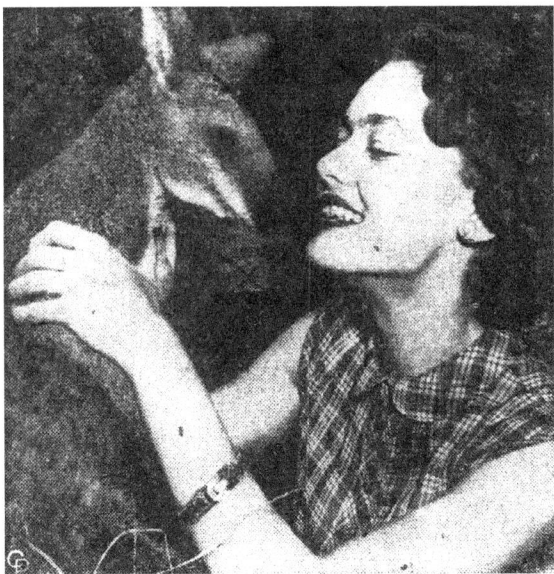

Fig. 1.12 Miss *Kangaroo*, Loretta North, and Joey

Fadden (1894–1973), and 20th Century-Fox's Australian publicity director, Hartley Stuart-Codde, they said the gift of a kangaroo was 'calculated to create a measure of favourable publicity to this country.'[260] And in June 1952, the Australian counterpart of Hopalong Cassidy, the country and Western singer Smoky Dawson (1913–2008), was due to show off a kangaroo named Zip at the 5000-seat Roxy Theatre in New York where *Kangaroo* was screening. But Zip escaped from Dawson's car on Long Island and eluded the search parties sent to find it. 'Now poor, frightened Zip is [reportedly] chowing grass on a millionaire's estate,' Keith Dunstan (1925–2013) of *The Herald* said. 'Newspapers are running stories on his escapades. Twentieth Century Fox people say that it's no publicity stunt, but, even so, they agree it is a very fortunate occurrence.'[261]

David F. Zanuck insisted on shortening *Kangaroo* from two hours, the director's cut, to 84 minutes, the final cut.[262] 'He can be good, but boy oh boy, he can also be very, very bad,'[263] Lewis Milestone lamented. Typical of most critics' lukewarm reviews of the film was the assessment by B.G. of *The Age*: 'A second sight of the film only confirmed my impression after the preview—that *Kangaroo* is about the calibre of a Western—and not a particularly good one at that.'[264] However, I feel they missed something. One of the very few critics who did "get" *Kangaroo* was Jane Corby of *The Brooklyn Eagle*:

> *Kangaroo*, stimulating Australian-made outdoor action film, starring elemental forces—drought, bush fires, sandstorms—and natural actors, including kangaroos and frogmouth owls. Story and human actors take only second place in interest. Had all the charm of novelty for me. Nominally a melodrama, the story *Kangaroo* tells, in Technicolor, doesn't interfere with the travelogue aspects—doesn't even begin to compete in visual fascination with the untamed natural forces of Australia, whenever they are unleashed on the screen. Neither, I don't hesitate to add, can the excellent cast, headed by Maureen O'Hara and Peter Lawford, compete with kangaroos sailing over the ground or stampeding cattle hardly glimpsed at all behind clouds of thick yellow dust. *Kangaroo*, in fact, [...] is a dramatic movie form for which we have no adequate name. [...] So, while *Kangaroo* has to be called a melodrama, because it has the basic melodramatic structure, it actually represents a new theatrical type, which has been appearing with increased frequency and which tells a thread of often trite story, as *Kangaroo* is posed against overwhelmingly interesting backgrounds. It isn't quite correct to label *Kangaroo* a "melodrama with travelogue aspects" because it is more than that. Its story, though a typical Western in plot, and one that has seen a lot of use besides, becomes as good as new because here the tale outclassed by its strange setting, seems to grow out of and be indigenous to the striking locale.[265]

In my view, *Kangaroo*'s cast and crew discovered the difference between an American Western and an Australian Western the hard way—through lived experience. At first blush, the easiest way to make an Australian Western seemed to be by simply swapping the prairie for the bush, a cattle ranch for a cattle station, a ranch house for a homestead, cowboys for stockmen, Native Americans for Aboriginals, coyotes for dingoes—and kangaroos(!), rattlesnakes for tiger snakes, 20th Century Fox for Ealing Studios, Bel Air for Zanuckville, and so on. But it was much more complex than that, not to mention the influence of being far from Hollywood, feeling like an outsider, the harsh climate, the primitive working conditions, and the cultural and economic differences between America and Australia. However, in the process, the result was not only different but, in some respects, more interesting than the original. What distinguishes *Kangaroo* from most American Westerns of the era is its emphasis on a sense of place and overcoming adversity instead of merely action and violence.

NOTES

1. 'Power to Come Here for Film?' *The Sunday Times* (Western Australia), 28 November 1948, p. 3.
2. Edwin Schallert, 'Ruth Roman Will Star as Doctor; Power May Miss *Australian Story*,' *The Los Angeles Times* (California), 8 May 1950, p. 66.
3. Jack Davies, 'Films Blamed for Crime Wave,' *The Daily Telegraph* (New South Wales), 6 February 1949, p. 43.
4. 'Reviews of New Films in Sydney,' *The Sydney Morning Herald* (New South Wales), 2 October 1949, p. 28.
5. David Bongard, 'In *Kangaroo* Lewis Milestone tells of "Land Down Under,"' *The Daily News* (California), 22 May 1952, p. 28.
6. 'US Films May Be Made Here,' *The Sydney Morning Herald*, 20 August 1950, p. 27.
7. Max Brown, *Australian Son: The Story of Ned Kelly*, Melbourne: Georgian House, 1948.
8. Max Brown, *Wild Turkey*, Melbourne: Georgian House, 1958, p. 12.
9. Max Brown, 'Horses, Horrors, Roos,' *The News* (South Australia), 9 January 1951, p. 9.
10. 'Reviews of New Films in Sydney.'
11. Thomas F. Brady, 'Columbia Holding *Born Yesterday*,' *The New York Times* (New York), 3 June 1949, p. 21.
12. Thomas F. Brady, 'Warners Acquires Play by Fay Kanin,' *The New York Times*, 7 June 1950, p. 34.

13. 'Giving *Kangaroo* an Australian Accent,' *The Daily Telegraph*, 13 August 1950, p. 63.
14. Charles Higham and Joel Greenberg, *The Celluloid Muse: Hollywood Directors Speak*, London: Angus & Robertson Ltd, 1969, p. 166.
15. 'Personal,' *The Advertiser* (South Australia), 21 August 1950, p. 2.
16. Herb Stein, 'Hollywood in Review,' *Philadelphia Inquirer* (Pennsylvania), 27 August 1950, p. 85.
17. Zelie McLeod, 'An Un-Hollywoodish Hollywood Man,' *The Daily Telegraph*, 30 September 1950, p. 21.
18. J. Griffen-Foley, 'Trouble-Shooter in a Headache Job,' *The Film Weekly* (Australia), 26 October 1950, p. 3.
19. 'Our Films are a Flop: Hayseed Themes, Miscasting, Miserly Budgets—That's Why,' *Smith's Weekly* (New South Wales), 16 September 1950, p. 7.
20. 'Two More Nights for *Kangaroo*,' *The Goulburn Evening Post* (New South Wales), 25 June 1952, p. 3.
21. 'Giving *Kangaroo* an Australian Accent.'
22. Charles G. Clarke, 'We Filmed *Kangaroo* Entirely in Australia,' *American Cinematographer*, July 1952, p. 292.
23. 'Hollywood Sees a Never-Never Land,' *The Advertiser*, 4 June 1952, p. 8.
24. Thomas F. Brady, 3 June 1949.
25. Henry Gris, 'Hollywood Report,' *The Sunday Herald* (New South Wales), 24 April 1949, p. 8.
26. 'Avenues for Australian Players,' *The Daily Telegraph*, 22 December 1949, p. 22.
27. 'English Actress for *Kangaroo*,' *The Age* (Victoria), 25 August 1950, p. 2.
28. 'Movie Man on Racial Films,' *The Sydney Jewish News* (New South Wales), 24 November 1950, p. 9.
29. 'Kangaroos Too Fierce for Local Film Men,' *Smith's Weekly*, 23 September 1950, p. 2.
30. Charles Higham and Joel Greenberg, p. 166.
31. *The Sydney Morning Herald*, 1 October 1950, p. 11.
32. Charles Higham and Joel Greenberg, p. 166.
33. Ibid.
34. Ibid., p. 167.
35. Zelie McLeod.
36. Blake Brownrigg, 'Movie Hero, Villain "Never Felt Fitter,"' *News*, 16 December 1950, p. 2.
37. 'Australian Aborigines Dance Rain-Making Corroboree for *Kangaroo*,' *The Film Weekly*, 26 June 1952, p. 16.
38. David Bongard.
39. Ibid.
40. Blake Brownrigg, 'Film Start Next Week,' *The News*, 12 December 1950, p. 2.

41. Charles G. Clarke, p. 292.
42. Norman Meares, 'Film Theme Suits Jubilee,' *The Advertiser*, 13 December 1950, p. 3.
43. Maureen O'Hara with John Nicoletti, *'Tis Herself: An Autobiography*, New York: Simon & Schuster Paperbacks, 2004, p. 272.
44. Ibid.
45. Ibid.
46. Charles G. Clarke, p. 315.
47. *The Sydney Morning Herald*, 24 April 1949, p. 48.
48. Lon Jones, '*Kangaroo* to be "Special" Film,' *The Advertiser*, 16 September 1950, p. 7.
49. Greg Rawson, 'English Stars in Big Australian Technicolor Film,' *The Sun* (Sydney), 17 August 1950, p. 37.
50. 'English Actress for *Kangaroo*,' *The Age*, 25 August 1950, p. 2.
51. Erskine Johnson, 'Hollywood,' *Park City Daily News* (Kentucky), 7 November 1950, p. 4.
52. Lon Jones, 16 September 1950.
53. Blake Brownrigg, 'S.A. Heat Worried Film Star,' *The News*, 8 March 1951, p. 13.
54. Maureen O'Hara and John Nicoletti, p. 273.
55. Ibid., pp. 143–144.
56. John L. Scott, 'Power Sees Odyssey "Pleasant, Profitable" Back in Brentwood Home, Tyrone Says He Realized Travel Ambition,' *The Los Angeles Times*, 20 November 1949, p. 105.
57. 'Milestone for *Kangaroo*,' *The Herald* (Victoria), 26 July 1950, p. 14.
58. 'Reviews of New Films in Sydney.'
59. 'Jean Simmons May Play in Film,' *The Advertiser*, 23 August 1950, p. 1.
60. Jack Davies.
61. 'Jean Simmons May Play in Film.'
62. Edwin Schallert.
63. Ibid.
64. 'Reviews of New Films in Sydney.'
65. 'Lawford Rushed: Stars Arrive in S.A.,' *The News*, 30 November 1950, p. 32.
66. William Latimer, 'Notes on Films: Steady, Girls, Here is Peter Lawford,' *The Sydney Morning Herald*, 20 August 1950, p. 26.
67. Ibid.
68. Ibid.
69. 'Dining and Dancing,' *The Truth* (New South Wales), 5 November 1950, p. 42.
70. '*Kangaroo* Stars Arrive,' *The Advertiser*, 1 December 1950, p. 3.
71. Charles Higham and Joel Greenberg, p. 190.

72. 'Film Stars Arrive in Port Augusta: Night Plane and Car Trip from Adelaide: Minor Banquet put on by Cookhouse Staff,' *The Transcontinental* (South Australia), 8 December 1950, p. 1.
73. 'Dinkum Aussies—All,' *The Sydney Morning Herald*, 15 October 1950, p. 34.
74. 'Finlay Currie's Rush Trip for *Kangaroo*,' *The Film Weekly*, 16 November 1950, p. 5
75. Gil Wahlquist, 'Actor Names Spencer Tracy No. 1,' *The News*, 2 December 1950, p. 5.
76. 'To Play Father in *Kangaroo*,' *The Mail*, 11 November 1950, p. 26.
77. '*Kangaroo* Stars Arrive.'
78. 'Equity May Declare Film Star "Black,"' *The Age*, 12 February 1951, p. 3.
79. 'New Opening to *Kangaroo* Planned,' *The Advertiser*, 24 February 1951, p. 3.
80. Maureen O'Hara and John Nicoletti, p. 273.
81. 'Maureen O'Hara's Big Sydney Welcome,' *The Film Weekly*, 30 November 1950, p. 5.
82. '*Kangaroo* Stars To Have Short Stay Here,' *The Advertiser*, 27 November 1950, p. 3
83. Blake Brownrigg, 'Maureen O'Hara's Life Story—Instalment 8: S.A. Heat Worried Film Star,' *The Barrier Miner* (New South Wales), 10 March 1951, p. 4.
84. 'Giving *Kangaroo* an Australian Accent.'
85. Hussein, 'The Screen: *Kangaroo* Hops Along All Right,' *The Southern Cross* (South Australia), 11 July 1952, p. 15.
86. 'Director Who Made Lordly Clifton Webb: Lewis Milestone Expected in Port Augusta Soon,' *The Quorn Mercury* (South Australia), 14 September 1950, p. 2.
87. Doug Easome, 'The Odd Spot,' *The News*, 7 November 1952, p. 3.
88. 'Chance to Play Second to Maureen O'Hara: Aust. Actress Gets Role in *Kangaroo*,' *The Daily Telegraph*, 3 December 1950, p. 7.
89. '100 Extras for *Kangaroo*,' *The News*, 29 August 1950, p. 17.
90. 'Local Girl Adds Colour to Film,' *The Victor Harbour Times* (South Australia), 25 July 1952, p. 3.
91. 'S.A. Horsewoman Thrills Film Unit,' *The Mail*, 24 February 1951, p. 13.
92. 'Film Horses for Sale,' *The News*, 28 February 1951, p. 2.
93. 'Film Job for Toorak Youth,' *The Herald*, 3 January 1951, p. 3.
94. Blake Brownrigg, 'Movie Hero, Villain "Never Felt Fitter,"' *The News*, 16 December 1950, p. 2.
95. Max Brown, 1958, p. 39.
96. 'Stars Fought Own Battle with Whips,' *The News*, 25 June 1952, p. 23.
97. Ibid.

98. Dudley Kemp, 'Kemp, Dudley,' https://gawlerhistory.com/Kemp_Dudley, accessed 16 December 2020.
99. Blake Brownrigg, 'Blood ... Sweat ... Tears,' *The News*, 15 December 1950, p. 13.
100. 'Drinking Tea as They Make Film,' *The Mail*, 18 November 1950, p. 9.
101. 'He Learned to Fall Down the Stairs the Hard Way,' *The Sydney Morning Herald*, 13 November 1950, p. 4.
102. 'Film Stars and Extras Go to Sea: Shots for Colour Film Taken Aboard MV Moonta: Passengers Drink Beer While Actors Endure Heat,' *The Transcontinental*, 2 February 1951, p. 3.
103. Mr. Pim, 'Passing By: Ants,' *The News*, 2 February 1951, p. 10.
104. *Valley Times* (California), 5 November 1951, p. 6.
105. Dudley Kemp.
106. 'Port Augusta People See Film Unit at Work: Scenes Enacted Near Sandy Creek Bridge,' *The Quorn Mercury*, 25 January 1951, p. 2.
107. '*Kangaroo* Shooting Postponed,' *The Advertiser*, 20 December 1950, p. 4.
108. Michael X. Savvas, 'Good Country: Port Augusta, Hollywood Outpost,' *The Adelaide Review*, issue 488, https://www.adelaidereview.com.au/latest/travel/2020/09/29/good-country-port-augusta-hollywood-outpost/, accessed 18 March 1921.
109. 'Milestone's Method of Movie-Making! Visuals Sketched for Every Scene,' *The Film Weekly*, 26 June 1952, p. 25.
110. Rita Dunstan, 'This Artist is Fast!' *The Argus*, 27 April 1951, p. 6.
111. Lon Jones, '*Kangaroo* Story Again Changed,' *The Advertiser*, 21 October 1950, p. 7.
112. '*Kangaroo* Australian Epic,' *Road and Home* (Australia), December 1951, p. 34.
113. Ibid.
114. 'Port Augusta Chosen as Main Base for the First Australian Colour Film: Company of 150 to be on Location for Four Months,' *The Quorn Mercury*, 24 August 1950, p. 1.
115. Mary Armitage, '*Kangaroo* Slept Here,' *The Film Weekly*, 14 December 1950, p. 34.
116. Ibid.
117. '*Kangaroo* Complete by February,' *The Advertiser*, 23 November 1950, p. 3.
118. 'Interest in Film Quickens: Port Augusta Plans to Help in *Kangaroo*,' *The Advertiser*, 25 August 1950, p. 3.
119. Jim Macdougall, 'Contact: Old Shades,' *The Sun*, 9 November 1950, p. 1.
120. 'Set for *Kangaroo*: Film Men to Build Home,' *The News*, 24 August 1950, p. 1.

121. 'Executives Satisfied. Quick Work in Planning Site of Film,' *The News*, 21 September 1950, p. 11.
122. R.M.E., 'Film Stars Not Coming Here This Afternoon: Will Leave Plane at Port Pirie,' *The Whyalla News* (South Australia), 1 December 1950, p. 1.
123. 'Site for Film Homestead "Pin-Pointed,"' *The Advertiser*, 30 August 1950, p. 3.
124. 'City Episode in New Colour Film: Sydney Probable Site,' *The Quorn Mercury*, 7 September 1950, p. 1.
125. R.M.E.
126. Blake Brownrigg, '*Kangaroo* Setting is Masterpiece,' *The News*, 14 December 1950, p. 36.
127. 'Homestead for Film,' *The Mail*, 21 October 1950, p. 2.
128. R.M.E.
129. L. McGovern, 'Biting Australia's Dust,' *The Sunday Herald* (New South Wales), 4 February 1951, p. 4.
130. Michael X. Savvas.
131. R.M.E.
132. 'Party Off to Film Site,' *The News*, 28 August 1950, p. 2.
133. 'Site for Film Homestead "Pin-Pointed."'
134. 'Big Lighting Plan for *Kangaroo*,' *The Advertiser*, 9 December 1950, p. 3.
135. Blake Brownrigg, 14 December 1950.
136. 'Film Homestead Taking Shape,' *The Advertiser*, 25 October 1950, p. 14.
137. 'Outdoor Shooting for *Kangaroo* Begins,' *The Mail*, 30 December 1950, p. 3.
138. Colton's, Advertisement, *The Advertiser*, 4 June 1952, p. 9.
139. Blake Brownrigg, 14 December 1950.
140. 'Film Men's Big Worry is Period Props,' *The Mail*, 30 September 1950, p. 7.
141. Jim Macdougall, 9 November 1950.
142. 'He Found Props for Film,' *The Mail*, 7 October 1950, p. 10.
143. Period & Art Furnishers, Advertisement, *The Advertiser*, 4 June 1952, p. 8.
144. Blake Brownrigg, 14 December 1950.
145. 'First *Kangaroo* Shots Tonight,' *The News*, 20 December 1950, p. 32.
146. Roberts Dunstan.
147. 'Producers Did Everything on a Grand Scale,' *The News*, 25 June 1952, p. 21.
148. Lawrie Jervis, 'The Odd Spot: Thorough,' *The News*, 18 January 1951, p. 3.
149. Heather Summerton, Email to Derham Groves, 14 March 2022.

150. 'Lawford Denies Film Stars Discontented,' *The Mail*, 9 December 1950, p. 3.
151. Blake Brownrigg, 'S.A. Heat Worried Film Star,' *The News*, 8 March 1951, p. 13.
152. 'First Scenes Shot for *Kangaroo*.'
153. Blake Brownrigg, 'Two Years' Planning went into 80-minute Film: Fine Outback Photography in *Kangaroo*,' *The News*, 25 June 1952, p. 20.
154. 'Site for Film Homestead "Pin-Pointed."'
155. Dudley Kemp.
156. 'Stars Fought Own Battle with Whips,' *The News*, 25 June 1952, p. 23.
157. 'Bite by Spider,' *The Brisbane Telegraph* (Queensland), 8 January 1951, p. 7.
158. Norman Meares, 'Film Work Delayed on *Kangaroo*,' *The Advertiser*, 11 December 1950, p. 3.
159. 'Wit at Stars' Reception,' *The News*, 1 December 1950, p. 3.
160. 'Film Men's Big Worry is Period Props.'
161. *Hollywood Comes to Australia*, http://bigstories.com.au/story/our-history/film/hollywood-comes-to-australia, accessed 4 May 2022.
162. 'Flies were Unhelpful Film Stars,' *The News*, 23 December 1950, p. 2.
163. 'Film Episode "Goes Up" in Whirlwind,' *The News*, 11 January 1951, p. 3.
164. Charles G. Clarke, p. 315.
165. L. McGovern.
166. Ibid.
167. 'Stars Fought Own Battle with Whips.'
168. '*Kangaroo* Australian Epic.'
169. 'Natives on Way to Film Site,' *The News*, 8 January 1951, p. 2.
170. '*Kangaroo* Complete by February,' *The Advertiser*, 23 November 1950, p. 3.
171. Max Brown, 'The Film Natives Are All Smiles,' *The Mail*, 27 January 1951, p. 2.
172. 'Film Lesson for Natives,' *The News*, 17 January 1951, p. 2.
173. Blake Brownrigg, 'Movie Hero, Villain "Never Felt Fitter."'
174. Blake Brownrigg, 15 December 1950.
175. Ibid.
176. 'Nasal Customs of Aborigines,' *The Advertiser*, 1 February 1951, p. 7.
177. 'Country Section: First Shots of Natives,' *The Advertiser*, 30 January 1951, p. 12.
178. Daniel Eisenberg, '"You Got the Wrong F***in Black Man!" The Indigenous Experience in the Australian Western,' in Cynthia J. Miller and A. Bowdoin Van Riper, *International Westerns: Relocating the Frontier*, Lanham, Maryland: Scarecrow Press, Inc., 2014, pp. 208–209.
179. 'Few Kangaroos Left in Australia, H'wood Finds,' *The Honolulu Advertiser* (Honolulu), 15 November 1950, p. 10.

180. Lon Jones, 'Inside Hollywood: Hollywood Insists on Kangaroos,' *The Advertiser*, 28 October 1950, p. 7.
181. Ibid.
182. 'S. Australian Kangaroos "Camera Shy,"' *The Newcastle Sun* (New South Wales), 10 January 1951, p. 5.
183. Lon Jones, 28 October 1950.
184. Norman Meares, 11 December 1950.
185. L. McGovern.
186. Lon Jones, 28 October 1950.
187. Charles G. Clarke, pp. 316–317.
188. 'Land "Down Under" Scene of Technicolor Film *Kangaroo* Starring Peter Lawford, Maureen O'Hara and Thousand Extras,' *The Decatur Daily* (Alabama), 22 June 1952, p. 6.
189. 'Australian Aborigines Dance Rain-Making Corroboree for *Kangaroo*,' *The Film Weekly*, 26 June 1952, p. 16.
190. David Bongard.
191. Special Correspondent, 'Abos. Quit Arc Lights for Mission,' *The Brisbane Telegraph*, 17 February 1951, p. 20.
192. 'S.A. Film's Boomerang Session.'
193. Isla Brook, 'This Week's Sydney Today: Bearded,' *The Mail*, 17 March 1951, p. 38.
194. Blake Brownrigg, 'Maureen Wants to Learn Native Dance,' *The News*, 12 December 1950, p. 9.
195. Robin Slessor, 'A Star Says Farewell: O'Hara's Fans Turn Tables, Give Her Autographs,' *The Daily Telegraph* (New South Wales), 25 February 1951, p. 10.
196. Ibid.
197. 'Film Natives Show Skill,' *The News*, 31 January 1951, p. 5.
198. Special Correspondent.
199. Gayne Dexter, 'The Movie Merry-Go-Round,' *The Truth*, 22 June 1952, p. 30.
200. 'Port Augusta Chosen as Main Base for the First Australian Colour Film: Company of 150 to be on Location for Four Months,' *The Quorn Mercury*, 24 August 1950, p. 1.
201. Charles G. Clarke, p. 293.
202. R.M.E.
203. Lon Jones, '*Kangaroo* Story Again Changed.'
204. 'Executives Satisfied. Quick Work in Planning Site of Film,' *The News*, 21 September 1950, p. 11.
205. 'Zanuck Says Thanks,' *The News*, 14 December 1950, p. 13.
206. 'Film Stars Welcomed,' *The Whyalla News*, 8 December 1950, p. 1.
207. Ibid.

208. R.M.E.
209. Ibid.
210. Jim Macdougall, 'Contact: Service,' *The Sun*, 11 December 1950, p. 1.
211. 'Lawford Denies Film Stars Discontented,' *The Mail*, 9 December 1950, p. 3.
212. 'Christmas Festivities at Zanuckville. Film Stars to Provide Entertainment. Maureen O'Hara in Singing Number,' *The Transcontinental*, 22 December 1950, p. 1.
213. 'The Queen of Zanuckville,' *The News*, 12 December 1950, p. 9.
214. Marion Follett, 'Maureen has Beauty & Charm of the Irish,' *Whyalla News*, 15 December 1950, p. 3.
215. Blake Brownrigg, 'Maureen, on Location, Talks About Home,' *The News*, 13 December 1950, p. 4.
216. Marion Follett.
217. Hills Hoist, Advertisement, *Advertiser*, 4 June 1952, p. 8.
218. 'Executives Satisfied. Quick Work in Planning Site of Film,' *The News*, 21 September 1950, p. 11.
219. 'Maureen O'Hara's Bed in Zanuckville Auction,' *The Advertiser*, 7 March 1951, p. 10.
220. Blake Brownrigg, 12 December 1950.
221. 'Important Preliminary Announcement: Clearing Sale, Saturday, March 17, 1951, 10 A.M. Sharp at Zanuckville, Port Augusta, Elder Smith and Co. Limited,' *The Transcontinental*, 9 March 1951, p. 2.
222. Ibid.
223. Blake Brownrigg, 12 December 1950.
224. 'Important Preliminary Announcement: Clearing Sale.'
225. R.M.E.
226. 'Film Scene in Temp. at 130,' *The News*, 29 January 1951, p. 19.
227. Max Brown, *Wild Turkey*, p. 48.
228. 'Reception at Film Colony,' *The Film Weekly*, 26 December 1950, p. 11.
229. 'Xmas in S.A.'s Little Hollywood,' *The News*, 23 December 1950, p. 14.
230. Ibid.
231. William Waymouth, 'Good Morning,' *The Advertiser*, 1 January 1951, p. 2.
232. 'Phone Box Xmas,' *The News*, 23 December 1950, p. 16.
233. Blake Brownrigg, 'Stars' Xmas Greetings,' *The News*, 15 December 1950, p. 4.
234. 'Phone Box Xmas.'
235. Norman Meares, 11 December 1950.
236. 'Musical Family Entertain Members Kangaroo Film Unit: "Hakendorfs Family of Which SA Should be Proud,' *The Quorn Mercury*, 18 January 1951, p. 3.

237. Ibid.
238. Norman Meares, 11 December 1950.
239. Michael X. Savvas.
240. 'Film Country Impresses Director,' *The Advertiser*, 6 December 1950, p. 3.
241. Blake Brownrigg, 'Film Start Next Week,' *The News*, 12 December 1950, p. 2.
242. 'Star Applauded at End of Show,' *The Transcontinental*, 26 January 1951, p. 1.
243. *The Rock Island Argus* (Illinois), 8 September 1950, p. 16.
244. 'Film Country Impresses Director,' *The Advertiser*, 6 December 1950, p. 3.
245. 'Film Artists to Referee Boxing,' *The Advertiser*, 19 January 1951, p. 7.
246. 'Boxing Tourney Attracts Big Crowd: 600 Patrons at Port Augusta Town Hall: G. Petrie Wins Trophy for Best Boy of Night,' *The Quorn Mercury*, 1 February 1951, p. 2.
247. 'Cowboy Boots for Boy,' *The Mail*, 3 February 1951, p. 8.
248. 'Wife of Film Man Shops with the Stars,' *The Sun*, 11 November 1953, p. 38.
249. 'Presented with Film Script,' *The Transcontinental*, 2 March 1951, p. 2.
250. 'Maureen Here Tonight,' *The News*, 23 February 1951, p. 1.
251. 'Triumph for Boone,' *The Quorn Mercury*, 26 June 1952, p. 2.
252. 'Maureen O'Hara's Bed in Zanuckville Auction,' *The Advertiser*, 7 March 1951, p. 10.
253. 'Over 1,000 at Film Unit Sale,' *The Advertiser*, 19 March 1951, p. 3.
254. 'Stockman Saves Calf in Gulf,' *The News*, 17 February 1951, p. 12.
255. 'Film Horses for Sale,' *The News*, 28 February 1951, p. 2.
256. 'Rent for Zanuckville Homes Reduced. Council's Overtures to Premier Successful,' *The Transcontinental*, 11 May 1951, p. 5.
257. Photograph, *The Marion Star*, 2 January 1952, p. 8.
258. Aline Mosby, 'Kangaroos Made Monkey of His Glamour-Girl Chaperone,' *The Brooklyn Daily Eagle* (New York), 16 May 1952, p. 9.
259. Photograph, *The Film Weekly*, 29 May 1952, p. 3.
260. Ibid.
261. Keith Dunstan, '*Kangaroo* Film "Horse Opera,"' *Newcastle Morning Herald and Miners' Advocate* (New South Wales) 7 June 1952, p. 5.
262. Ibid.
263. Charles Higham and Joel Greenberg, p. 168.
264. B.G., 'New Films: Fine Camera Work in *Kangaroo*,' *The Age*, 13 June 1952, p. 2.
265. Jane Corby, 'At the Movies: Roxy's New Picture Presents Maureen O'Hara, Peter Lawford,' *The Brooklyn Eagle*, 17 May 1952, p. 14.

CHAPTER 2

Hopalong Cassidy on Tour

Abstract This chapter is about the 1954 tour of Australia to raise money for "crippled" children by the American actor William Boyd, who played the cowboy, Hopalong Cassidy, on film, radio, and television. It looks at the public reception he received on arrival in Darwin, Northern Territory, especially from the Aboriginal population that included some of his biggest fans. It also examines the surprising influence of Cassidy on Aboriginal culture. It describes what Boyd did in Melbourne, Victoria, on 12 November 1954, beginning with his visit to the Royal Children's Hospital and ending with his appearance at Wirth's Circus, which caused a riot. Finally, this chapter looks at some Australian-made character merchandise produced for his visit, such as Hoppy Cola, the Hopalong Cassidy Game, and Hopalong Cassidy sweets.

Keywords Aboriginals • Australia • Character merchandise • Darwin • Disability • Hopalong Cassidy • Melbourne • William Boyd • Wirth's Circus

DARWIN AIRPORT

The American actor William Boyd (1895–1972) starred as Hopalong Cassidy, or "Hoppy" for short, the fictional American cowboy created by the American author, Clarence E. Mulford (1883–1956), in a series of popular American B-grade Western films between 1935 and 1948. In 1946, he purchased the commercial rights to the character from Mulford and the American film producer, Harry "Pop" Sherman (1884–1952), turning his old movies into a hit children's TV show and licensing hundreds of Hopalong Cassidy products around the world, including Australia. In November 1954, Boyd visited Australia and caused a sensation, the likes of which were not seen there again until the British pop group The Beatles (1960–1970) toured a decade later. Huge crowds greeted Boyd in Darwin, Melbourne, Adelaide, and Sydney during his 16-day visit to raise money for "crippled" children, most of whom had polio.[1] As with *Kangaroo: The Australian Story* (1952), discussed in Chap. 1, his trip was paid for with funds earned in Australia by his two US companies, William Boyd Enterprises and Hopalong Cassidy Enterprises, and "frozen" by the Australian government.

At 8:30 p.m. on Tuesday, 9 November 1954, Boyd and his glamorous fifth wife, Grace Bradley Boyd (1913–2010, m.1937–1972), aka "Tripalong" or "Trippy," arrived in Darwin, the capital of the Northern Territory, onboard a QANTAS Constellation Jetliner from Singapore. In those days, Darwin was a bustling frontier town that—at least in spirit— was similar to America's Wild West of a century earlier. One could hardly imagine a more fitting place for the world's favourite cowboy of books, comics, films, radio, and TV to begin his much-anticipated Australian tour. However, things got off to a bad start. The Boyds had left the USA on 8 July 1954, first to accompany 44 American newspaper boys to England for two weeks and then to travel on their own to Europe, the Middle East, Asia, and Australia (Fig. 2.1). As a result, by the time the 59-year-old actor stepped off the plane at Darwin, he was exhausted and in need of a rest. 'Sleep, just sleep,'[2] was all that Boyd wanted to do during his first 24 hours in Australia. 'I am not going to get much sleep for three days after I leave Darwin,' he correctly surmised. 'I intend to get some here.'[3] But when Boyd saw the huge crowd waiting to greet him at the airport, he quickly realised what it meant—nowhere near as much sleep as he hoped.

2 HOPALONG CASSIDY ON TOUR 51

Fig. 2.1 William Boyd (*centre*) and the 44 American newspaper boys about to depart for England

'More than 1000 Australians, Aborigines, Chinese, and Greeks jammed the road to the airport an hour before [Boyd] arrived,'[4] *The Sun News-Pictorial* reported. The multicultural crowd indicated not only Darwin's diverse population but also Hopalong Cassidy's universal appeal—almost everyone loved him! When Boyd emerged from the plane and walked down the gangway, his enthusiastic fans gave him 'one of the most tumultuous welcomes anyone has ever received in Darwin.'[5] The size and enthusiasm of the crowd caught the airport authorities off guard, as hundreds of 'men, women, and children and Aborigines with their children on their shoulders'[6] broke through the customs and quarantine barriers to be closer to their hero. The excitement was so infectious that even usually "sensible" newspaper boys were affected. 'Out at the aerodrome on Tuesday night, there was one exceptionally fanatical young Hopalong Cassidy fan,' *The Northern Territory News* said. 'He was one of our newsboys, and our newsboys always watch their coin. Nonetheless, this fellow dumped his papers and his money-tin in the drome lounge foyer, and joined the crush, caring not at all about his wealth.'[7]

Despite being shocked by all the people at the airport to meet him, Boyd smiled, waved, blew kisses, and "shot" children using his index finger and thumb like a gun and they yelled even louder. (He had to use make-believe guns because his famous pair of pearl-handled six-shooters had been impounded by Australian Customs officials a week earlier and had not yet been returned to the movie star.) 'The reception has staggered me,' Boyd declared. 'I decided to take a day off in Darwin to get some sleep. I could have done better and hidden myself away in Sydney.'[8]

Nothing they had told Boyd about Darwin tallied with what he saw. Consequently, he felt deceived and—rightly or wrongly—blamed Tom Harris, the owner of Star Pictures, the only cinema in Darwin, who was looking after the Boyds during their stay in town. 'I thought this was a one-pub town. That's why I stopped off for a day. I expected a couple of children to meet me, but [...] nothing like the reception I got. [They] told [me] there were only a few hundred people in Darwin, but I saw many more than that when I stepped off the aircraft.'[9] Uncharacteristically, Boyd asked, 'How can I get out of here without giving too many autographs?'[10] It was not Boyd's finest hour. While he was usually easy-going, he also could be very prickly—as on this occasion—but it is worth remembering that it was Hopalong Cassidy, the cowboy, who was larger than life and not William Boyd, the actor!

Many Aboriginals who met Boyd at Darwin airport had travelled a long way under treacherous conditions to get there. For example, one Tiwi Island family had sailed 20 kilometres from Melville Island to the mainland in a paper-bark canoe and then walked 40 kilometres to the airport.[11] Another Tiwi Island family had sailed 60 kilometres from Bathurst Island to Gunn Point, a peninsula northeast of Darwin, in a tiny dugout and then walked 70 kilometres to the airport while carrying their best clothes with them to change into on arrival.[12]

Boyd's Aboriginal fans elected Aboriginal elder Alice Leydin as their spokesperson. 'I welcome you to our country,' she told him. 'You do a lot of good.'[13] He responded by giving her a Hopalong Cassidy good luck token.[14] I believe that Aunty Alice's "official" welcome was a very early—if not the very first—modern-day welcome to country ceremony (i.e., a speech or performance of welcome by an Aboriginal elder at the start of a public event). The well-known Aboriginal performers, actor Ernie Dingo (b.1956) and musician Richard Walley (b.1953), claimed to have "invented" the concept in 1976.[15] But Aunty Alice beat them to it by 22 years.

Fig. 2.2 Two sides of a Hopalong Cassidy good luck token

The 30-millimetre diameter aluminium tokens Boyd liberally handed out to his fans had Hopalong Cassidy's head on one side and a four-leaf clover, a horseshoe, and a wishbone on the other side (Fig. 2.2). He had shipped 10,000 of them to Australia on the S.S. *Ventura*, but a wharfies' strike had delayed their delivery. Following talks between Boyd's American manager, Robert Stabler (1918–1988), and the General Secretary of the Waterside Workers' Federation, "Big" Jim Healey (1898–1961), the strike ended earlier than expected so Boyd would have the tokens in time for his arrival in Melbourne, the capital of Victoria—such was the screen cowboy's influence. 'Those [tokens] have given us more trouble than any urgent cargo,'[16] Healey said.

Aunty Alice adopted the surname of her employer, Reg Leydin (1905–1993), the Government Secretary of the Northern Territory (1948–1952, 1953–1954, 1963).[17] He played an instrumental role in the infamous "Petrov Affair," the only other event in Darwin in 1954 to rival Hopalong Cassidy's visit.[18] On 19 April 1954, the Moscow-bound plane carrying Dusya Petrov (1914–2002), the wife of the Russian spy Vladimir Petrov (1907–1991), who had just defected to Australia, and her two Russian Secret Service KGB captors who looked like 'a couple of mobsters from a third-rate gangster film,'[19] arrived in Darwin from Sydney. Mrs. Petrov's future looked grim, but while they refuelled the plane at the airport, Reg persuaded her to defect with her husband.[20] His diplomatic coup was an embarrassing slap-in-the-face for the Soviet Union, the Cold War enemy of the Free World. Consequently, they promoted Leydin to be Administrator of Nauru (1954–1958, 1962–1966), a South Pacific island 4200 kilometres northeast of Darwin, which resulted in Aunty Alice losing her job.[21]

When William Boyd had finished talking to the crowd at the airport, the police escorted him and his wife to Tom Harris' car, whence they drove to the Hotel Darwin, the best in town. He was now even more spent than when he had landed—and no wonder. Despite his bluster, Boyd had "met" more than 1000 children in less than two hours after arriving in Australia. 'He shook hands with more than 300 people, wrote 250 autographs, and kissed at least 20 of the young girls,[22] *The Courier-Mail* said.

'Don't let anybody disturb me tomorrow,' Boyd told the hotel staff. 'Tell them anything. Tell them I have gone bush, but don't let anybody near my room.'[23] Boyd also told Harris he would not be making any personal appearances in Darwin.[24] 'I must preserve my strength,' he argued. 'I can't possibly fulfill every request as I have a big program in the south of Australia.'[25] But now that Boyd had seen for himself just how much Darwin's First Nations Australians, in particular, loved Hopalong Cassidy, it was easy for Harris to persuade him 'to visit the schools and the natives, his most ardent fans, the next day.'[26] Tired as he was, he could hardly disappoint them now.

Among the eager crowd to welcome Hopalong Cassidy to Australia at Darwin airport was the local bush poet Bill Armbrust, whose poem "The Coming of Cassidy" captured the hectic events of that evening brilliantly:

> I took a drive on Tuesday night
> And joined the happy throng,
> Of a thousand other Darwin folk
> Who welcomed Hopalong.
> I made the Darwin airport
> With an hour or two to spare,
> And was trampled flat beneath the feet
> Of the people waiting there.
> The yelling of the children
> And the cheers on every hand,
> Gave ample warning that the plane
> Was just about to land.
> It seemed a little foolish
> That grown men, big and strong,
> Should be waiting there like children
> Just to see old Hopalong.
> So I went around and borrowed
> My cobber's little boy,
> And I lined up at the airport

Just as gay and just as coy,
As any other Hoppy fan
Who came from far and near.
And I joined in with the others
When they gave old Bill a cheer.
And there was good old Hoppy,
With smiles for all the throng
Coming marching down the gangway
With his pretty Tripalong.
And Tommy Harris waited there
With a smile upon his face,
To give the Western hero
A welcome to our place.
And so I pushed and shoved and squeezed,
And trampled on the kid.
I wouldn't go through that again,
Not for a hundred quid.
And Hoppy got a good idea
What Australian cattle are,
As he battled through a thousand head
On the way into his car.
And when our hero rode away
In triumph through the scrub,
I grabbed my toddler by the ear
And dashed off to the pub.
To find, alas, that it was closed
To me and to the kid,
So Hoppy you unwittingly
Have saved me half a quid.[27]

DARWIN SCHOOLS

The Boyds' second day in Darwin (Wednesday, 10 November 1954) also began badly. 'Autograph-seekers and amateur photographers woke the movie star at the Hotel Darwin this morning,'[28] *The Newcastle Morning Herald and Miners Advocate* said. When hotel staff delivered two glasses of pineapple juice to their room at 9:00 a.m.,[29] William Boyd told them he was unavailable before 11:00 a.m.[30] Besides some well-deserved R&R, he may have tried to catch up on some business, as local manufacturers of Hopalong Cassidy products wanted to contact him. One was George Aitken, Managing Director of the Australian Record Company, which produced several Hopalong Cassidy records starring Boyd. Aitken had written to Boyd to offer his assistance. He also told him they were about to release a new record, "Hopalong Cassidy and the Sheep Rustlers" (1954), but they did not wish to detract from his main objective, to raise money for children with polio.[31] Other local manufacturers of Hopalong Cassidy merchandise faced the same dilemma.

Despite having been woken early, Boyd was in a far better mood than he had been on the previous night at Darwin airport and happily signed autographs for the 'steady trickle of children,'[32] who dropped by the hotel to see him. He also spoke to a journalist from *The Sun-Herald*. 'While I was sitting with Hoppy in a hotel drinking lemon squash, an official asked him whether he would see one of his most ardent fans,' he said. 'He introduced [Aboriginal elder] Tipperary [Tilipoura], a cleaner at the courthouse, who has never missed a Hopalong film. They talked together. Then Tipperary felt Hoppy's arm and said, "You don't need any guns—you very strong."'[33] Boyd presented him with a Hopalong Cassidy good luck token.[34] Uncle Tipperary was not a cleaner but a major-domo at the courthouse. 'If he didn't like the look of you, he wouldn't let you inside,'[35] said Ted Egan (b.1932), an Australian folk musician and former Administrator of the Northern Territory (2003–2007).

In the afternoon, Tom Harris collected Boyd and Phynea Paspalis, the 11-year-old daughter of Michael Paspalis, the proprietor of the Hotel Darwin and co-owner of the Star Pictures cinema, to take them to her primary school, St Mary's Convent. Darwin resident Geoff James thought Frank Wise (1897–1986), the Administrator of the Northern Territory at the time (1951–1956), loaned Harris a car to ferry Boyd around town.[36] It was either a Ford Customline[37] or a Land Rover[38] (there were conflicting memories about its make). Boyd's black Hopalong Cassidy outfit was with Robert Stabler in Sydney, so he wore a white safari suit instead. While some fans were possibly disappointed to see him dressed in civvies, his cowboy costume was probably too uncomfortable to wear in the humid climate of Darwin anyway. It appears that Boyd's wife, Tripalong, stayed at the hotel.

At St Mary's Convent, Boyd addressed a school assembly in his usual breezy style, telling everyone 'I love you all.'[39] Former student Terence Cody remembered him standing next to the nuns on the school's verandah,[40] and Phynea Paspalis remembered him performing a magic trick with one of his tokens.[41] Boyd also visited some individual classes at the convent. 'Hopalong Cassidy came to our class, and the first bloke he saw was me, and he gave me a hug,'[42] former student Arthur Que Noy told me. He was eight years old and a big fan of Hoppy's movies, which he regularly saw at Star Pictures on Wednesday nights, its weekly "Western Night." Another pupil, five-year-old Leslie Kilmartin, was wearing a cowboy hat and holding a toy pistol. Boyd pointed his index finger and thumb at him, but he "fired" first. 'I got you, Hoppy,'[43] Kilmartin yelled excitedly.

Next door at St Mary's Presbytery, a nun borrowed a Kodak Six-20 Brownie to photograph Boyd with some of his fans, including Aboriginal elder Matthias Ulungura (1921–1980). He was well known for capturing Sergeant Hajime Toyoshima (1920–1944), a World War II Japanese fighter pilot who crashed his warplane on a remote part of Melville Island, 107 kilometres north of Darwin, on 23 February 1942. Uncle Matthias sneaked behind him, told him to "Stick 'em up," took his gun, and marched him to the nearest police station a day's walk away.[44] Tom Harris retold the story six months later at a Rotary Club dinner in Portland, Victoria, explaining where Uncle Matthias learned the expression, "Stick 'em up." 'I can claim something in that little episode,' the cinema owner claimed. 'You see, he had been to my pictures and had seen Hopalong Cassidy in action.'[45] Over the years, Ted Egan heard Uncle Matthias' account of capturing Toyoshima several times, which confirmed the unlikely role of his screen hero. He told the Japanese airman to 'Stickem-up, allasame Hopalong Cassidy,'[46] according to Egan. Uncle Matthias was not only a big fan of Hoppy but also his comic sidekick, "Windy" Halliday, played by George Hayes (1885–1969) in 14 films between 1935 and 1939. So, he was very disappointed when Hayes did not come to Australia, too, even quizzing Boyd about it. 'What's wrong? You didn't bring Windy,'[47] Uncle Matthias asked (Fig. 2.3).

Egan met Boyd at St Mary's and thought he patronised the Indigenous men he met, 'patting them on the head and saying things like "Hi there boy,"'[48] which was regrettably common then but is unacceptable today. Be that as it may, Boyd was vehemently opposed to racism and segregation in the USA. For example, one time he appeared at a department store in the Deep South, he was concerned that black and white children were standing in separate lines, Grace Bradley Boyd recalled many years later.

> When he asked why […] he was told there were two lines because the black kids were going to have to wait and come last. And Bill said, 'The kids come in together and they come in equal, or I'm not coming in at all.' It was a tense situation because segregation was apparently a deep-seated tradition

Fig. 2.3 William Boyd (*centre*) and Matthias Ulungura (*right*) at St Mary's Presbytery

with that particular store, but they knew there would be a riot if Hoppy didn't appear as promised, so they had to give in. Some of the black children and their parents were within earshot when Bill was facing off with the store manager, and I will never forget the looks on their faces. They were so thrilled that Hopalong Cassidy was standing up for them, and I'm sure it's something they remembered for the rest of their lives, just as I have.[49]

Closer to home, Tom Jones of Melbourne radio station 3UZ asked Boyd, 'Have you already found that the character of Hopalong Cassidy has a place in the hearts of young people outside the British-speaking section of the world? For example, are there coloured boys who know about Hopalong too?' Chuckling, Boyd said: 'We just came out of Ceylon the other day, and practically all there are coloured boys. You see, to Hoppy, there is no colour. Every little boy, every little girl, every man, and every woman is the image of God, and God had no colour. We don't recognise colour, languages, religions—they're just wonderful people. The coloured people feel the same towards Hoppy as Hoppy feels towards them.'[50]

His next stop was Darwin Primary School. Children in grades one to three went to the campus at Frogs Hollow, and children in grades four to six went to the campus in Woods Street, which Boyd visited first. Former students John Waters recalled him talking to the children about his horse Topper (1935–1961), and Vic Streatham remembered him giving the children the rest of the day off school, which annoyed the teachers.[51] Then Boyd was going to Frogs Hollow until a teacher said something to upset him. 'I vividly recall Mr. Boyd saying in a loud voice, "Come on Tom, no damn schoolteacher is going to tell Hopalong Cassidy what to do,"' Waters said. 'And with that, he headed for his car—with a sheepish Tom Harris in train.'[52] Children mobbed Boyd as he walked through the schoolyard, former pupil Ernie Chin recalled. 'You could not get near him! He stopped to give a girl named Pat Wayne a good luck token. We were so envious!'[53] As Boyd drove away, 'one of the boys could not contain his joy and jumped onto the running-board of the car,' said Geoff James, another former pupil. 'The Headmaster, Mr. Cant, pulled him off and gave him a whack. Hoppy stopped the car, got out, and chastised the headmaster for hitting the boy.'[54] In the meantime, the other children, unaware that Boyd had cancelled his visit in a huff, were excitedly waiting for him to arrive. When he failed to show up, they were devastated. 'I remember the tears of the grades one, two, and three children who had missed out, coming up from Frogs Hollow, some with their Mums,'[55] Waters said. Greg Tonks was one of the bitterly disappointed Darwin Lower Primary students who didn't get to see Hoppy that afternoon. 'The Headmistress, Miss Cameron, bought each boy a Dinky toy car and each girl a little doll to make us feel better,'[56] he recalled.

At St Mary's Convent and Darwin Primary School, 'the children fired question after question at the film star, and the girls blushed or tried to duck for cover each time Hoppy announced, "I must get a kiss from the prettiest gal in the room before I leave,"' *The Courier-Mail* said. 'They asked him what had happened to his horse Topper, where he had left his guns, and questions about his film partners Windy and "California" [Carlson, played by Andy Clyde (1892–1967)]. Before Hoppy left each school, he posed for photographs with the children—native and whites.'[57] The children must have felt like he had stepped off the screen and into their classrooms.

Finally, Boyd visited the Bagot Road Native Reserve at Ludmilla, seven kilometres north of Darwin's Central Business District (CDB).[58] As some of his biggest fans lived there, 'it was a pity that only about 30 were present due to the short notice of his visit,'[59] *The Courier-Mail* said. In 2014, Aboriginal elder Don White remembered meeting Boyd like it was only yesterday:

That picture fella, Hopalong Cassidy! Oh yeah! We didn't know until the last minute that he was coming to visit us. We were all waiting for him on the basketball court and then a car pulled up—we thought he might come on his horse! We were too frightened to speak. He was the first movie star we'd ever met. We lined up for him and he shook everyone's hand. Incredible! My goodness! He was number one![60]

Hopalong Cassidy was the favourite screen cowboy of Aboriginals, Tom Harris said. 'Some natives are never seen in town except when there's a Hopalong Cassidy film on,' he told *The Sun-Herald*. 'I show about a dozen Hoppy films a year. Some are repeats, but the natives don't mind.'[61] It seems Harris also told this story to the Boyds because in *Hopalong Cassidy: An American Legend* (2008) by Grace Bradley Boyd, she tells a more colourful version of it:

> A theatre had been built especially for [the Aboriginal people] where every Sunday they could see a motion picture, and the first picture they ever saw happened to be a Hoppy. Well, they absolutely loved it, so the people running the theatre said okay, if Hoppy makes them happy, we'll give them another one next week. So they all came next Sunday and they nearly tore the place down because they didn't want a different Hoppy, they wanted the same one again. That incident had happened two years before we got there and they were still showing the same picture every Sunday because that's the only one they'd accept.[62]

Such was the racism in Darwin in 1954, the only day that Aboriginals were permitted in town after 8:00 p.m. was Wednesday (not Sunday, as Grace Bradley Boyd said), which also happened to be Western Night at the Star Pictures cinema. According to Uncle Don White, the Department of Native Affairs sent a big, canvas-sided truck to Bagot Road Native Reserve to collect the Aboriginal men, women, and children who wanted to attend.[63] If they were fortunate, a Hopalong Cassidy film was showing. Eric Jolliffe (1907–2001), an English-born Australian cartoonist best known for his humorous depictions of Australian outback life (many of which would be considered nowadays as tasteless—if not racist), described a night when they showed a Hoppy film:

> Past the box-office file notorious killers by spear and magic, warriors, stockmen, horse breakers, crocodile hunters, buffalo shooters; men whose tracking ability and knowledge of the wilds and wild life make them without peer;

artists of the paintbrush and corroboree; all turn briefly from a life that is wilder and more spectacular today than ever the vaunted Wild West was in its heyday. For tonight they ride with Hopalong and his fellows.[64]

As Boyd's last day in Darwin was a Wednesday, they screened *Borrowed Trouble* (1948) starring Hopalong Cassidy, Andy Clyde, and Rand Brooks (1918–2003), who played "Lucky" Jenkins, another of the sidekicks, at Star Pictures that night.[65] A reporter for *The Sun-Herald* asked 'a strapping young tribal Aboriginal named Jimmy' there, who he liked best? 'Hopalong Cassidy—he number one,' he replied. 'Hopalong ride horse good!'[66] Jimmy probably knew what he was talking about, as many Aboriginal men were expert stockmen.

The influence of Hopalong Cassidy on Aboriginal culture during the 1950s is surprising to say the least. Motion pictures were known as '"Hopalongs," thanks to the infiltration of Mr. Cassidy,' Gayne Dexter of *The Sun-Herald* claimed.[67] Hoppy also dogged the making of the Australian film *Jedda* (1955), directed by the Australian filmmaker Charles Chauvel (1897–1959). It was about the cultural and racial tensions between three young Aboriginals caught in a tragic love triangle: Jedda, an Aboriginal girl adopted by a white couple and raised on their remote cattle station in the Northern Territory, was played by Ngarla Kunoth (1927–2022). Marbuck, an Aboriginal outlaw wanted for murder, who belonged to a different tribe than Jedda, was played by Robert Tudawali (1929–1967). And Joe, a hardworking stockman with an Afghan father and an Aboriginal mother, who worked for Jedda's parents, was played as a child by 12-year-old Willie Farrar and as an adult by Paul Reynall. When Chauvel first asked Tudawali to appear in *Jedda*, he did not understand what he wanted him to do until he explained, 'You Hopalong Cassidy.'[68] When Chauvel and his wife Elsa (1898–1983) visited Tudawali after making the film, he explained how he lost all of the money he had earned from it. 'His relatives and those of Peggy, his wife, came to him. "You Hopalong Cassidy now," they said. "You got plenty of money." So, he shared it with them.'[69] When Willie Farrar turned up on location one day in a Hopalong Cassidy sweater, he could not understand why the director would not let him wear it.[70] Chauvel also had to keep a supply of Australian-style hats, shirts, trousers, and boots for the Aboriginal stockmen to wear in the film instead of their own 'Hopalong Cassidy stuff.'[71] Indeed, he was so concerned by the Americanisation of Aboriginal stockmen that he asked the Association of Australian Graziers to do something about it.[72]

Between 1949 and 1955, the American comic book illustrator, Dan Spiegle (1920–2017), drew the Hopalong Cassidy comic strip, which appeared in newspapers worldwide, including in Australia. A few months before Boyd's visit, Dan Grayson, the American President of Hopalong Cassidy Enterprises, commissioned Spiegle to draw a comic strip set in Australia. For background, he borrowed some books about Australia from the Melbourne toy manufacturer, Alex Tolmer (1914–1998), who made Hopalong Cassidy cap guns in Australia.[73] Grayson also asked John Hick, an employee of Personality Merchandising, the Melbourne company that licensed Hopalong Cassidy character merchandise in Australia, to "Australianise" the comic strip's dialogue.[74] 'I hope it meets with the readers' approval in Australia,' Grayson later told Tolmer. 'We have tried very hard to get an authentic Australian story out of the deal.'[75] In it, Hoppy tracks a gang of horse thieves from San Francisco to Sydney, where he encounters a tribe of hostile Aboriginals. Until Boyd visited Darwin in 1954, nobody in his inner circle knew how much First Nations Australians idolised Hopalong Cassidy. Otherwise, I am sure Spiegle would not have depicted him fighting them while dodging their boomerangs and spears.

Around midnight, the Boyds boarded a QANTAS Constellation Jetliner for Melbourne via Sydney. Due to the late hour, only about 50 people were at Darwin airport to farewell them. William Boyd gave Hopalong Cassidy good luck tokens to two children there, 'telling them they should not be up so late and [… to] go to bed,' *The Northern Territory News* reported. In *Hopalong Cassidy: An American Legend*, Grace Bradley Boyd described the joy of Darwin's Aboriginal population at meeting Boyd/Hoppy in person and the special parting gift they gave them: 'They were in a state of complete awe. I've never seen such a thing before or since because it was worship, just absolute worship. As we were leaving, they gave us a kangaroo foot for protection, and good luck, which we learned was a very special gesture on their part.'[76] But she was thinking of their Melbourne farewell, I believe, since it was Lady Jacobena Angliss (1896–1980), the President of the Children's Welfare Association of Victoria, who presented them with a kangaroo foot/paw—although it had a cigarette lighter mounted on the end of it! The Melbourne goldsmiths James W. Steeth & Son, makers of the Melbourne Cup, produced the expensive gift. Reflecting on their visit to Darwin at Sydney airport before heading to Melbourne, Boyd said:

We dropped into Darwin on Monday [sic] night and I got the surprise of my life. We were tired and needed a rest, and we planned to have a quiet day in Darwin before we flew on down here. I thought Darwin was just an airport with a little country hotel. When I looked out of the aeroplane, there were two or three thousand kids [sic]—gosh, you should have seen 'em. And they all wanted Hoppy, so Hoppy it had to be. You know what? Some of those kids had come 200 and 300 miles [sic] to see Hoppy. Next day, instead of resting, Hoppy went to the Catholic school, then to the public school, and then to the school where a lot of wonderful little Aboriginal kids—they were the most wonderful of the lot, and they knew all about Hoppy. It was a full day, and no rest, but the kids had to have Hoppy.[77]

ROYAL CHILDREN'S HOSPITAL

William Boyd was even busier in Melbourne, Adelaide, and Sydney than Darwin. For example, the following is a detailed account of what he did on Friday, 12 November 1954—his first full day in Melbourne and the first time he dressed as Hopalong Cassidy in Australia. It vividly illustrates his hectic schedule and, more importantly, how popular he was in particular, and cowboys were in general, in Australia during the 1950s.

At 9:45 a.m., Boyd left the Windsor Hotel in Spring Street, Melbourne, for the Royal Children's Hospital in Pelham Street, Carlton, two kilometres away, accompanied by Robert Stabler.[78] Mrs. Boyd remained at the hotel. A note scribbled on Boyd's itinerary indicated she and Lady Jacobena Angliss were to visit a sheep farm.[79] However, there was a change of plan because at the Victorian School for Deaf Children, later that afternoon, he said she was still in bed![80] Boyd and Stabler drove to the hospital in a black Zephyr convertible, imported from England by the Ford Motor Company for Boyd's visit. Ken Wise was a schoolboy in Geelong, 72 kilometres southwest of Melbourne, where Ford had its factory. His friend's stepfather (Mr. Baily) worked there and had road-tested Boyd's car before they delivered it to him. 'He loaded us in the Zephyr and drove us all around Geelong in Hopalong Cassidy's car,' Wise recalled. 'Coz I was Hopalong Cassidy "mad," I was so excited about it! I told everyone at school that I'd been in Hopalong Cassidy's car. I had never been in an open car before. I remember telling my schoolmates there were holsters in the upholstery for his guns, which I made up!'[81]

'Thousands of children from nearby schools packed the pavements outside the hospital and screamed their welcome as the Western hero arrived,'[82] *The Daily Mirror* reported. One was Silvana Cattapan, a pupil at St George's Catholic Primary School. Viewing the scene from Grattan Street, she was moved by the sick children lined up on the hospital's open verandahs, patiently waiting for Boyd to arrive. Cattapan's family had only recently migrated to Australia from Italy, so she spoke very little English and knew nothing about Hopalong Cassidy. Nevertheless, her classmates' excitement at seeing their cowboy hero in person was so infectious, she was just as thrilled as they were—whoever he was![83] About 400 mothers and children had also assembled right outside the hospital's entrance to catch a glimpse of Boyd before he went inside. 'Hi little chickens,' he said, stepping from his car. A large group of children quickly surrounded him in order to look at his famous pair of Colt 45s. 'No, no bullets,' he said. 'We have to save those ... we may run into a bad man.'[84]

Inside, Boyd went from bed to bed, speaking to the young patients. One-year-old John Secombe had eczema and was crying in his cot.[85] But as soon as Boyd picked up the youngster, his tears stopped. 'Must be the mother in me,' he joked. A photograph of them, cheek-to-cheek, was published in *The Sun News-Pictorial* the next day.[86] When Boyd gave six-year-old Paul Hill a Hopalong Cassidy good luck token, the pleased-as-Punch patient flashed a toothless grin that reminded him of his curmudgeonly old sidekick, Windy Halliday (George Hayes).[87] 'For heaven's sake, you guys, what ya doin' here?' Boyd asked 9-year-old Robert Christie and 13-year-old Hugh Gardiner, who had almost recovered from their illnesses and were nearly ready to go home. 'You look like you ought to be out playing football,'[88] he said.

Hopalong Cassidy's pearl-handled revolvers were a big hit with the patients, particularly the boys. 'I don't know what it was about me, but he came over to me, sat on the bed, and showed me his two silver guns,' recalled Allan Rouse. 'I held them, and they took a photo of us, which filled half a page in *The Sun News-Pictorial* the next day [13 November 1954, p. 19]. When my mother opened the newspaper and saw it, she was surprised because she hadn't been to visit me for a week and knew nothing about it. She contacted the paper, and they sent her a copy of the photograph. I still have it sitting on our mantelpiece.'[89] Boyd asked 12-year-old Roy, bedridden for six months, '"Hell pardner, how're these women [i.e., the nurses] treatin' you?" Then Hoppy lifted one of his long-barrelled six-guns from a holster and handed it to the boy. "Some gun, boy, isn't it?" he said.'[90]

After badly burning his leg, Paul Haar was in and out of hospital for two years. 'I was scheduled to go home on "leave" the day before Hopalong Cassidy was due to visit the hospital,' he said. While his parents and the hospital staff encouraged him to stay one more day so he could meet his cowboy hero, he chose to go home instead. 'I have regretted it ever since,' Haar lamented nearly 60 years later. 'The choices a 6-year-old makes!'[91] Cassidy could cheer up children—sick or otherwise—like few other celebrities could. Consequently, the medical staff said they had never seen their patients so happy. 'This is as good as a tonic for the kids,' one doctor said about Boyd's visit. 'Our primary purpose is to treat them, but we can only treat them properly if they are happy.'[92]

As Boyd had been playing Hopalong Cassidy for a long time (since 1935), his fans included not only children but also adults. Two nurses—one in a mask and gown ready for surgery—and three doctors—one smoking a cigarette and two with their hands in their pockets—were photographed rubbernecking at him. Furthermore, the doctors were absentmindedly blocking the view of a small boy (Fig. 2.4).[93] After the photograph of the "guilty" trio appeared in the press, they received a

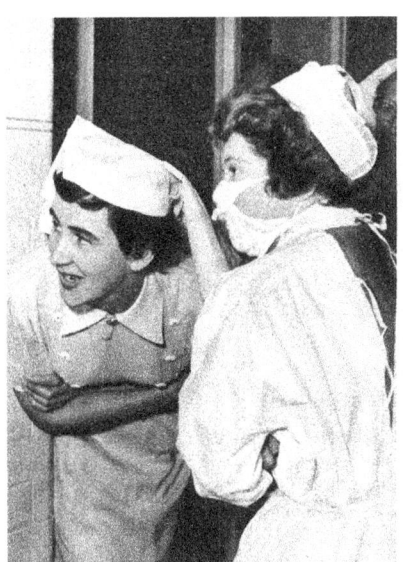 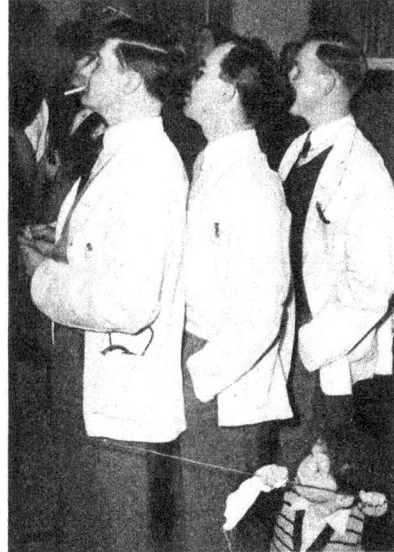

Fig. 2.4 Royal Children's Hospital staff craning to see Hopalong Cassidy

terrible ribbing from their friends, the widow of one of the doctors told me.[94] The photos of the staff looking at Boyd instead of looking after their patients inspired a wonderful cartoon by WEG (aka William Ellis Green, 1923–2008) in *The Herald*. It showed six doctors dressed in surgical masks and gowns and holding scalpels and bone saws, gawking at the famous cowboy instead of operating on a small boy who was already prepped and receiving blood. 'Go on, gawk at Hopalong!' he protested. 'Forget about my polyoxymethylene sorbitol agene!'[95]

YOORALLA

William Boyd left the Royal Children's Hospital around 11:00 a.m. for Yooralla, a school for disabled children located nearby in the same street.[96] In 1954, most of the children at Yooralla had polio, short for poliomyelitis, a cruel, muscle-wasting, infectious disease. Victims whose legs were affected had to wear braces or callipers to walk, while those whose chest muscles were affected had to live inside a tank respirator known as an "iron lung" to breathe. Polio was a worldwide scourge until a vaccine developed by the American virologist Dr. Jonas Salk (1914–1995) became available in 1955.

Eagerly waiting for Boyd to arrive at Yooralla was nine-year-old Barney McLees, a polio victim from Albury, 326 kilometres north of Melbourne. 'On his crutches, Barney stood alone inside the entrance gate as Hoppy drew his guns and grim-faced advanced. [When] he reached the boy, he laughed, bent down, and kissed his cheek,'[97] *The Sun News-Pictorial* said. Inside, Boyd handed out Hopalong Cassidy good luck tokens and signed autographs. Almost 60 years later, Margaret Cooper still treasured the souvenir token he gave her and the slip of paper on which he scrawled, 'Good Luck, Hoppy.' As Cooper was '"horse crazy,"' she was disappointed that Boyd had not brought his white stallion, Topper.[98] However, horses from the USA had to be quarantined for at least six months on arrival, making it virtually impossible for Topper to have accompanied his master. Furthermore, Australia's strict quarantine regulations meant they held the Olympic equestrian events in Stockholm instead of Melbourne in 1956.[99]

When Boyd gave a good luck token to a pretty little girl named Kay, the eight-year-old boy standing next to her pulled out his toy cap gun and aimed it directly at the film star. In the best tradition of cowboy movies, he warned Hopalong Cassidy to 'back off' because Kay was *his* girlfriend.

Fig. 2.5 Ben Lewin (*centre*) pointing his toy gun at Hopalong Cassidy

The young gunslinger, Ben Lewin (b.1946), had contracted polio two years earlier, aged six (Fig. 2.5).[100] Coincidently—or perhaps not—he became a filmmaker in Los Angeles. Lewin's credits include the acclaimed TV series *The Dunera Boys* (1985), starring Bob Hoskins (1942–2014), and the feature film *The Sessions* (2012), starring Helen Hunt (b.1963). He still walks with the aid of crutches due to catching polio.

'I met Hopalong Cassidy face-to-face and was overjoyed to receive a lucky silver token from his hand,' recalled Peter Freckleton, a 'polio kid' at Yooralla. 'The memory hasn't gone, although, sadly, the token has!' According to him, Boyd's 'wonderfully benign and happy presence' at the school was a welcome relief from the excruciating remedies the polio victims had to endure, which in his case involved being in a whole-body Thomas splint for hours on end. 'It was torture, really,'[101] he said. In *The Yooralla Story 1918–1977* (1978), the author Norman Marshall 'blamed' Boyd for starting a trend at Yooralla in 1954. 'Hopalong Cassidy was one of the first of many celebrities and VIPs to visit and almost inundate Yooralla in the years to come,'[102] Marshall said. His use of the word 'inundate' suggests a degree of irritation with the school's high-profile visitors over the years. However, Boyd's visit didn't merely cheer up the students for an hour or so but left them with pleasant memories that have lasted over 60 years.

Victorian School for Deaf Children

William Boyd returned to the Windsor Hotel at noon for lunch. According to his itinerary, he was supposed to leave at 2:15 p.m. for the Victorian School for Deaf Children in St Kilda Road, Prahran, five kilometres southeast of Melbourne's CBD. However, he was running almost an hour late.[103] Anxiously waiting for Boyd at the school were 300 disabled children from three different local organisations: the Blind Institute, the Crippled Children's Society, and the Victorian School for the Deaf (Fig. 2.6). They kept his visit quiet to avoid a large crowd of curious onlookers at the school, although the press was present and reported the event the next day.[104] Their stories were painfully sentimental. 'Whatever their handicaps, the children sensed the moment their hero swept into the school drive in his shining open car,' *The Argus* said. 'Spontaneously, they burst into rounds of cheers as Hoppy stepped from the car and walked towards them. It was one of the great moments of their lives. And Hoppy did nothing but increase their happiness. He had a kiss or a hug for every one of the 300, and his laughing quips brought a smile to many tear-dampened cheeks.'[105] Gulp!

Boyd greeted the children and handed out Hopalong Cassidy good luck tokens. Susan Fry, a 13-year-old blind girl, ran her fingers over Boyd's face. 'My, but you're handsome!'[106] she told the actor, who was old enough to be her grandfather. Another blind girl named Lorna asked

2 HOPALONG CASSIDY ON TOUR   69

Fig. 2.6   Hopalong Cassidy arriving at the Victorian School for Deaf Children

Boyd to 'Take off his Hoppy voice.' When he continued to talk as he had done before, she joyfully exclaimed, 'But you're just the same!' '"That's right, honey," Boyd replied. "I'm Hoppy—and Hoppy is me."'[107] They introduced Boyd to two deaf children with familiar surnames: 13-year-old Fay *Boyd* and 14-year-old John *Cassidy*. The actor wrapped his arms around the two youngsters and declared, 'Here's the whole Cassidy family.' Then the happy trio posed for newspaper photographs. 'We noticed that he won't let the blind children think they can't see, nor the deaf children think they can't hear,'[108] a doctor told *The Herald*. Several deaf students later wrote about Boyd's visit in the school's magazine, *The Deaf Children's Chronicle*. For example, the following is Janice Nixon's report of her encounter with the movie star:

> On November 12th Hopalong Cassidy came to visit our school. The blind and crippled children came to our school, too. He went to the front lawn. We cheered him. He is a nice man, and he wore cowboy's clothes. Then

Hopalong gave a medal of himself to every child, and he kissed some of us. He kissed and hugged me, but I was shy. Then Hopalong went to Mr. Hansford's lounge room, and he had afternoon tea. [G.E. Hansford was the superintendent of the school from 1943 to 1956.] The dailies went home early, but the boarders didn't. We waited for him to come out. He had written his autograph for Mr. Hansford. I was jealous of him because he had the autograph. We cheered Hopalong again. I liked him very much.[109]

The Victorian School for Deaf Children presented Boyd with a book of newspaper cuttings about his Australian trip, compiled by the school's public relations officer, Emerald A. Goetze. As he had been in Australia for only four days, she apologetically and jokingly wrote 'incomplete at that'[110] on the front cover. Later, Boyd singled out his visit to the school as one of the highlights of his trip:

> It has me by the heart, this rip-roaring loving welcome which is everywhere. The people in the hotel, in the streets, and above all the children, particularly the deaf and blind children I met today, have given me the most wonderful experience of a lifetime. My first message of welcome was written in Braille from a little girl, and it will make Melbourne live forever in my heart. I'll be back some day if I can make it. I want to stay longer and see more of this great country.[111]

WIRTH'S CIRCUS

William Boyd departed the Victorian School for Deaf Children at 4:45 p.m. to appear in a special episode of *The Bunkhouse Show*, a half-hour Country and Western radio programme sponsored by Bonnington's Irish Moss cough mixture and broadcast nationally on the Macquarie radio network.[112] Members of the public were encouraged to pre-purchase tickets for five shillings each and come along to the show:

> This is a hold-up folks! For a very worthy cause. Come along and bring the kiddies to meet me—Hopalong Cassidy—in person at Wirth's Circus, Batman Avenue, on Friday, Nov. 12, at 5 p.m., when I'll be appearing in 'The Bunkhouse Concert' with such outstanding entertainment personalities as Lily Connors, Charles Tingwell, [who played Matt in *Kangaroo* (1952),] Noel Judd, Keith Walshe, The Bunkhouse Orchestra, The Harmony Twins, The Purtzel Sisters, The LeGarde Twins, Tex Baines' Hayseeds, and Tom Campbell's Orchestra.[113]

Initially, they planned to hold *The Bunkhouse Show* starring Hopalong Cassidy at the West Melbourne Stadium in Dudley Street, North Melbourne, two kilometres northwest of the CBD, which could seat 10,000 people. However, they changed the venue to Wirth's Circus tent at Gosch's Paddock, a large tract of vacant land in Richmond, three kilometres southeast of the CBD, which could seat 6000. The reason may have been because they had sold only 5000 tickets in the fortnight before the show.[114] As it turned out, neither the stadium nor the tent was big enough for the crowd that came to see Boyd in person. 'Queues began forming in Swan Street at 2 p.m.,' *The Age* said. 'By 4.30, they stretched to the Punt Road corner, 300 yards away, and underneath the Punt Road viaduct. At 4.45, all seats were taken, and many people were standing inside the marquee. But an estimated 8000 were still outside clamouring for admission.'[115]

Two Wirth's Circus performers, acrobat Lorraine Perry and bareback rider Leo St Leon, vividly recalled the crowd there on 12 November 1954. 'You couldn't see any of the grass for people. They were like ants, just wall-to-wall people on the lawn,'[116] Perry said. 'All you could see were these little kids in their black and white cowboy suits coming down with their parents. It was like a black and white invasion! They were coming from the tram stops, the bus stops, and the parking lots. It was amazing,'[117] St Leon recalled.

Boyd arrived at Wirth's Circus around 5:00 p.m. and went to the dressing-room tent via a rear entrance.[118] Maybe it was nerves or the cups of tea he had at the Victorian School for Deaf Children, but he needed to use the lavatory. The circus' whip-cracker, Ian Westbrook, later erected a sign in the toilet to commemorate the "historic" occasion: 'Hoppy pissed here.'[119]

The Sun News-Pictorial said that Boyd's arrival at the circus caused a 'near-riot.'[120] However, Perry was in no doubt whatsoever: 'It was a riot,' she said. 'You see all these screaming teenagers at these rock concerts? Well, that's what it was like. "Oh, Hoppy, Hoppy!" they were all yelling. The mums and dads were just as bad!'[121]

When the people queuing for over two hours to buy tickets finally got tired of waiting, they rushed inside the tent *en masse*. Then when the people who had tickets saw what was happening, they also charged inside the tent. It was mayhem. Eight-year-old Trevor Parkes was one of the hundreds of people who crawled under the flaps of the circus tent without buying a ticket. 'In those days, you lived on your wits and your rat cunning,'[122] he said, reflecting on working-class life in Melbourne in 1954. To prevent people from rushing into the tent, they used two circus elephants to block the two main entrances, but to no avail, as the crowd just ran around them. A cartoon by WEG in *The Herald* depicted the hapless pair of circus elephants on crutches and swathed in bandages: 'That's the last time I'll try to stop kids from seeing Hopalong!'[123] one elephant said to the other.

Inside the tent, the gate crashers filled the vacant seats reserved for disabled children and refused to budge. While those people without reserved seats stood around the ring, blocking the view of those sitting behind them. They ignored many requests to sit down on the ground so everyone could see the stage, prompting 'loud and bitter complaints [...] from all sections of the crowd,'[124] *The Sun News-Pictorial* reported. 'You could not have fitted a sardine in the tent, as there were so many people there,' Lorraine Perry said. 'The seats were full, so thousands of people and their kids were standing between the seats and the ring.'[125]

Eight-year-old Ray Johnson and his grandmother were in the alcove where the performers waited before going on stage, chatting to Country and Western singers The LeGarde Twins, waiting for their cue. 'They had a flask and were sipping from it. "What's that?"' Johnson asked. 'That's glycerine, son, to make our eyes shine!'[126] one of the twins replied. Next, to Johnson's surprise, Boyd entered the alcove and lifted him. 'I was just like a stunned mullet. I couldn't talk!' he said. 'Hopalong Cassidy didn't have his hat on, and I was shocked because his hair was silver-grey! But he should have had white hair—the same as his horse Topper! I've dined out on that story about Hopalong Cassidy picking me up for years!'[127]

Boyd rode a white mare named Goldie into the circus ring, recalled Tom Dumpleton, the roustabout who saddled the horse for him.[128] Boyd had once owned a share of Cole Brothers Circus in the USA, so he had done this sort of thing before. 'The lights would go down with a dramatic drum roll, and the spotlight would hit the entrance just before Bill came trotting in on Topper,' Grace Bradley Boyd said. 'They would make a slow circle around the outer edge of the arena, with Hoppy waving and doffing his black hat to the crowd.'[129] Although, Boyd's circus entrance in Melbourne failed to impress at least one young fan. 'As a typical city kid of that time, I was "cowboy mad,"' Grant Aldous said.

> Aged six and living in Kew East, [an affluent suburb, eight kilometres east of the CBD,] my mother got two tickets to go to his show in the big tent. I remember being taken there in the family's Morris Minor. But more intensely, I remember the bitter disappointment of seeing an ageing cowboy

ride around the arena waving to the crowd. In the eyes of a nipper, expecting the excitement of a shoot-out, there was little showmanship. But for some reason, I have clung to this memory and tell myself that at least I saw the man in the big black hat.[130]

When Boyd reached the stage at the centre of the ring, the crowd's behaviour became even worse. 'I think The LeGarde Twins came on and sang a song—or something like that—but the moment Hopalong Cassidy came on, everybody just got up and stampeded toward the stage,' Leo St Leon said. 'They just got up as one and moved forward like a giant wave. I said, "My God, look out, he's going to be run over by all the little magpies [i.e., the children wearing their black and white Hopalong Cassidy cowboy suits]!"'[131]

'As Boyd [...] climbed to the stage, people converged on him,' *The Age* reported. 'Children wearing cowboy outfits and carrying toy guns were held aloft to see the film star. Other children were knocked over by hysterical adults. The crush about the stage got completely out of hand as Hopalong began to talk to the crowd and reach out to the children nearest him.'[132] Trevor Parkes had fought his way to the front of the stage and managed to touch Hopalong Cassidy's shiny black boots. Boyd noticed the youngster and bent down to give him a black plastic woggle shaped like a steer's head. 'People tried to take it off me,' Parkes said. 'That's what happened in Richmond in those days. If somebody wanted something you had, he just took it off you. So I stuck the woggle on my index finger, made a fist, and put my hand in my pocket to keep it safe.'[133]

According to Lorraine Perry, Boyd planned to speak to the children from the stage. 'But he was in the ring only a few minutes before they had to get him out. It was the shortest appearance I'd ever seen.'[134] Circus attendants frantically tried to hold back the crowd, as Boyd called for calm. '"Hey, hey, hey," he said, in a low fatherly tone of reproof. But it was no use. They kept right on yelling at him. And Hopalong made the best of it. He called out "Hi" again in a friendly kind of greeting that brought more roars. Finally, he told the crowd he intended to do his broadcast show [...] in the tent, "but if you don't sit down, ah just can't do it here," he said.'[135] But it made no difference because they couldn't hear him. Wirth's antiquated public address system, consisting of 'a couple of speakers fixed to the side of a van parked at the rear of the tent,' could not compete with the din.[136] 'Six amplifiers were drowned in the confusion,' *The Age* said. 'Efforts by radio technicians to install others were thwarted by the crush of people jamming the tent'[137] (Fig. 2.7).

Fig. 2.7 William Boyd (*arrow*) calls for calm at Wirth's Circus

Then all hell broke out. 'They managed to get Hoppy into the middle ring of the circus tent,' said Perry. 'Then everyone jumped out of their seats and over the ring fence and charged him. People from Wirth's Circus quickly grabbed him and got him into the big empty lions' cage in the ring. "This will protect him," they thought. "He's got a big high cage around him." But when the people surged, those at the front were squashed against the cage. So, some fast-thinking person shouted over the microphone, "Quick, Hoppy's gone out the front of the tent." There were so many people in the tent they couldn't see him, so they thought, "Oh, Hoppy's gone out the front." And when they ran out the front of the tent to see him, the circus people grabbed him and took him out the back and put him in his car.'[138] A report in *The Age* graphically described the mayhem:

> Weeping women and children were knocked over and men fought in a hysterical crush inside the big tent. [...] Four crippled children, including one on a stretcher, had to be lifted over the heads of the crowd to safety behind the stage. [...] Many women fainted and several men fought openly. Sawdust from the ring floor was hurled at officials endeavouring to protect small children being buffeted and trampled in the struggle for vantage points. With the position dangerous, the police ordered the organisers to abandon

the show. The crowd refused to leave until Hopalong announced he would drive around the parklands in his car. There was an immediate rush to go outside and another crush developed near the exit behind the stage. Cars parked near the tent were damaged by people clambering over them to see Boyd leave. Cages housing animals served as grandstands.[139]

Outside, they kept the circus animals in cages, like a little zoo. People could look at the lions, tigers, and more, but they still had to keep their distance. So, after the crowd streamed out of the tent in hot pursuit of Boyd, 'most of the circus roustabouts tried to keep people out of the zoo area for fear someone got badly hurt,'[140] Dumpleton said. To return to *The Age* report:

> Boyd was mauled and had his cowboy outfit torn in the struggle to reach his car. Although protected by police and circus officials, he took 20 minutes to move 40 yards. [...] All Swan Street traffic was haltered as Boyd's car edged through the throng on to the road. On police orders the car left the area as quickly as possible with dozens of youngsters running behind it as far as Olympic Park, where it was able to accelerate in lighter traffic. About 40 children separated from their parents in the wild scenes inside the tent were later claimed.[141]

Cousins nine-year-old Terry Guest and seven-year-old Ross Clark were among those who chased Boyd's car as it left Gosch's Paddock. 'We had broken free somehow—things were different then, you could do what you wanted to do—and we charged after the car,' Guest said. 'When we got to it, Hoppy sort of put his hand out of the window, and I grabbed hold of it with great glee and gave it as good a shake as I could while my cousin kissed him through the car window!'[142] Next day, radio presenter Tom Jones quizzed Boyd about the circus fiasco on Melbourne station 3UZ:

> Well, that one I don't actually like to talk too much about. The thing you mean, of course, is the thing at the circus yesterday. I do know, personally, that they sold 5000 tickets. But they seemed to forget that Hoppy had a lot more friends than they thought he had. And Hoppy's friends seemed to be very enthusiastic friends. They want to get as close as they can, because the only place they've ever seen me is on a piece of paper, as a comic strip character; they want to see if you're real. Well, unfortunately, about 8000 more people broke through, which created practically a panic. And I want to say to the people of Australia who were there yesterday, and the children who

were there yesterday, that I'm quite sure you know the main purpose for coming here was to help the crippled children, not make cripples out of children. I was very upset about it. I did pray to God last night none of them were hurt, because that I wouldn't want. I want the friendship. I want the respect. I want the admiration and the enthusiasm. But I don't want harm to come to anyone.[143]

The shenanigans at Wirth's Circus were the low point of Boyd's trip to Australia. The ugly and violent behaviour of the crowd belied the easy-going, fair-minded, law-abiding, picture-perfect society most Australians believed they had in 1954. Indeed, it was fortunate nobody was seriously injured or killed. On the other hand, the "Felliniesque" image of elephants standing sentry amid the chaos is priceless. While undoubtedly shaken by what had just happened, Boyd still had one more commitment. Six-year-old John McDonald from Heidelberg Heights, 13 kilometres northeast of the CBD, hadn't been able to get to Melbourne Airport on Thursday morning to see Hopalong Cassidy arrive. So, *The Argus* had arranged for him to meet Boyd at the Windsor on Friday evening. 'As young Johnnie climbed onto Hoppy's knee, pulled on the cowboy's famous black sombrero, and brandished a gleaming six-shooter, he beamed: "Gee, this is a beaut."'[144] Thankfully, it was a quiet ending to a very hectic day.

Merchandising

William Boyd earned a lot of his income from the royalties he received for a wide range of Hopalong Cassidy products, such as bedspreads, cowboy suits, greeting cards, lunch boxes, pens, watches—you name it, he endorsed it![145] Since manufacturing was a highly protected industry sector in Australia following World War II, the Hopalong Cassidy products sold in Australia also had to be made in Australia. Some of my favourite examples are the soft drink, "Hoppy Cola," the parlour game called the "Hopalong Cassidy Game," and sweets, such as "Hoppy Belt Pouches," "Hoppy Pops," "Hopalong Cassidy Bar 20s," and "Hopalong Cassidy Ranch Toffees."

In 1954, Keith Harris & Co. Ltd., an Australian manufacturer of food colourings and flavours, was granted licences to produce Hopalong Cassidy cake decorations, Hopalong Cassidy cake frills, Hopalong Cassidy paper serviettes, and by far its most promising prospect, Hoppy Cola. They hoped it would rival Coca-Cola and Pepsi Cola in Australia. The new soft drink had an eye-catching red and white label featuring Hoppy riding

Topper. Also, its bottle cap resembled a Hopalong Cassidy Crippled Children's Appeal badge, hundreds of thousands of which the general public purchased leading up to Boyd's tour to raise money for charity. In January 1955, sales of Hoppy Cola were looking very good, Boyd's man in Australia, Larry Cleland, told Robert Stabler.[146]

The company planned a full-on advertising campaign for Hoppy Cola that included a radio commercial recorded by William Boyd. It also considered using any left-over Hopalong Cassidy good luck tokens—which Boyd handed out to his fans—to promote Hoppy Cola and, if they worked, then minting more locally. However, the advertising campaign was not as big as the company had hoped because the independent bottlers around Australia who produced the cola were reluctant to contribute to its cost. Consequently, some bottlers went ahead on their own, individually advertising in local newspapers. For example, Sheekey's Ltd. of Wagga in country New South Wales ran a series of ads in the *Daily Advertiser* that declared: 'Now—the drink you've been waiting for, "Hoppy Cola," the perfect kola flavour. It's new! It's delicious! Serve it cold. The whole family will love it. See Hopalong and Trigger on every label. Now on sale everywhere. Bottled by Sheekey's Ltd., Wagga.' Of course, every young would-be cowboy in Australia in 1954 could have told them that Topper was Hoppy's horse while Trigger belonged to his screen rival Roy Rogers.

Although, the ultimate downfall of Hoppy Cola was not due to poor advertising but poor quality. Keith Harris did not produce Hoppy Cola per se but rather the concentrate used to make it. The company sold this to over 50 bottlers throughout Australia, which made Hoppy Cola using their particular methods and techniques, then distributed it to grocery shops, milk bars, and so on, in their local areas. With so many bottlers making Hoppy Cola, Keith Harris could not monitor the quality and consistency of the soft drink produced. Even the designs of the bottles and labels could vary from one bottler to another. For example, the Hoppy Cola bottled by W.H. Moyle & Co. of Port Pirie, South Australia, had tall clear glass bottles and square labels. But that bottled by Cosgrove & Co. of South Brisbane, Queensland, had short brown glass bottles and rectangular labels. Since Keith Harris & Co. Ltd. had no control over production, it wanted a clause concerning the satisfactory performance of sub-contractors deleted from its licensing agreement with William Boyd to protect them from being sued. They understood the problem but could not fix it. One angry consumer even complained to Boyd himself about 'a well-known drink factory [...] selling dirty dishwater in bottles to children

Fig. 2.8 Hoppy Cola bottle

called "Hopalong" and telling [them] there is a motorcar prize for the lucky number. It's the biggest take for kids and charity, so please look into it.'[147] In 1959, Keith Harris did not renew its licence to produce Hoppy Cola. Not only had the soft drink sold far below expectations, but the Hoppy craze was well and truly over by then anyway (Fig. 2.8).

Between the 1900s and the 1970s, W. Owen Pty. Ltd. manufactured National-brand board games at its factory in Ballarat, 100 kilometres northwest of Melbourne. In 1954, it began making the Hopalong Cassidy Game under licence. Production was aligned with Boyd's tour of Australia, as the following advertisement aimed at potential local retailers indicates: 'An entertaining new National Game just in time for Hopalong Cassidy's visit. Don't miss the wonderful sales of Hopalong Cassidy games. Order your stocks now at all wholesalers.'[148] Two, three, or four players could play the game, which involved capturing outlaws and collecting reward money, as the rules explained (Fig. 2.9):

Fig. 2.9 Hopalong Cassidy Game manufactured by W. Owen Pty. Ltd.

Hopalong Cassidy, the County Sheriff, has been told that there are outlaws hiding in the nearby hills. Rewards up to $12,000 are offered for the capture of some of these desperadoes. Hopalong sends a posse, comprised of a number of deputies (2 for each player), to bring in these law-breakers: (taking them prisoners, bringing them into the Sheriff's office, and collecting the reward money). The game board represents the wild country where the action takes place. The centre of the board is the Sheriff's office with Hopalong Cassidy himself pictured there. The corners of the board show the hideouts where the bandits are hidden. Between the Sheriff's office and the hideouts, many trails lead in all directions. These trails are followed by the posse to round up the bandits and bring them to Hopalong's office.[149]

In America, Milton Bradley produced the Hopalong Cassidy Game. Between 1950 and 1956, it sold 635,000 games.[150] By comparison, between 1954 and 1958, W. Owen sold only 30,000 games, although over a third of them went during Boyd's 16-day visit, which was still pretty impressive.[151] While the Australian and American versions of the game were the same to play, there were several differences in their design due to a desire to reduce production costs in Australia. For example, the Australian-made game had a thin cardboard game board with nothing on the back, while the American-made one had a thick cardboard game board with a red paper and a silhouette of Hoppy riding Topper on the back. The Australian-made player pieces consisted of tiny coloured wooden blocks, while the American-made ones consisted of small, coloured, plastic figures of cowboys on horseback. The wooden blocks would have been cheaper to produce than the plastic figures. The Australian-made game used a plain box-and-die, while the America-made one used a red plastic arrow mounted on a square of cardboard, with images of Hoppy in each corner. The box-and-die would have been cheaper to produce than the spinner. Both versions of the game had coloured cardboard tokens to represent the bandits. Although, the Australian-made ones were square while the American-made ones were round, once again for economy of production. Printed on the lid of the game's cardboard box was the new "Official Hopalong Cassidy Trade Mark" logo. However, the Australian Trade Marks Office had concerns about it because, in its view, the word "official" cast doubt on the authenticity of earlier Hopalong Cassidy merchandise. Boyd's people consulted the Melbourne patent attorney, Clement Hack & Co., for advice, which resulted in some Australian licensees receiving small refunds.[152] But it didn't seem worth the fuss.

As children were Hopalong Cassidy's biggest admirers, it was not surprising that the Melbourne confectioners, Fyna Foods Pty. Ltd. and Bester's Sweets Pty. Ltd., wanted their products to be associated with him. After all, his young fans' pocket money was just as good as anyone else's. Fyna Foods, founded in the 1940s, was best known for making sherbet, a sweet fizzy powder consisting of mostly icing sugar, popular with children. Beginning in 1954, they produced several sweets named after Hoppy: "Hoppy Chews," a candy bar in four flavours. "Hoppy-Ade," a powder mixed with water to make a sweet fruit-flavoured drink. Toffees on sticks called "Hoppy Ringsticks," which came with an adjustable ring featuring Hoppy and Topper. "Hoppy Pops," described as 'Two Sweets in One ... Lolly Pop and Sherbet ... Dab the Pop in the Sherbet.' And "Hoppy Belt Pouches," three ounces of hard candy made to 'keep indefinitely in all climates,'[153] in a cardboard pouch, 78 x 50 x 150 millimetres, decorated with Hopalong Cassidy, a pair of six-shooters, and stirrups. As several

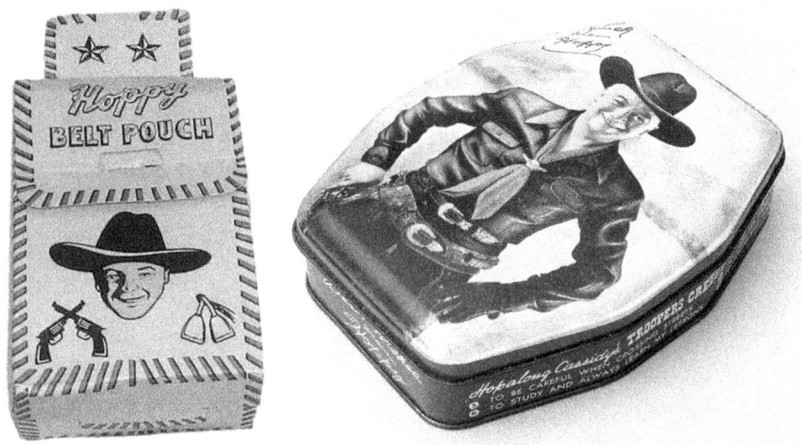

Fig. 2.10 Hoppy Belt Pouch (*left*) and Hopalong Cassidy Ranch Toffees tin

Australian chain stores were interested in selling them, Fyna Foods placed an initial order for 100,000 pouches, confidently adding 'this figure will be doubled or trebled.'[154] However, not many have survived, and they are as scarce as hen's teeth (Fig. 2.10).[155]

Fyna Foods gave away Hopalong Cassidy swap cards with Hoppy Pops and Hoppy Chews. The first series comprised 36 cards, showing Hoppy in the Wild West. For example, card number 16 had a colour drawing of him shooting a rattlesnake on the front and the following caption on the back: 'The rattlesnake is one of the deadliest reptiles found in the West. On his tail is the rattle that gives him his name. Before he strikes, these rattles vibrate rapidly, making a loud buzzing sound. The skin, when tanned, makes beautiful belts.'[156] The second series comprised 22 cards depicting scenes from the Hoppy film *Sinister Journey* (1948), and the third series also had 22 cards showing scenes from another Hoppy film, *Silent Conflict* (1948). The company offered to exchange 36 cards from series one for six Hoppy postcards and one autographed photo of Hoppy, 22 cards from series two for just the six postcards, and 22 cards from series three for just the autographed photo. In this way, children could redeem their duplicate swap cards for more giveaways, while the company could put the unwanted swap cards back into circulation.

In 1954, Bester's Sweets started making two types of Hopalong Cassidy candy: Hopalong Cassidy Bar 20s, a chocolate-coated macaroon candy bar in a bright yellow paper wrapper, and Hopalong Cassidy Ranch Toffees, individually wrapped toffees in an octagonal-shaped tin. On the lid was a photo of Hoppy, and on the sides was 'Hopalong Cassidy's Troopers' Creed for Boys and Girls,' which declared:

> To be kind to birds and animals.
> To always be truthful and fair.
> To keep myself neat and clean.
> To be courteous.
> To be careful when crossing streets.
> To study and always learn my lessons.
> To obey my parents.
> To avoid bad habits.[157]

The company launched Hopalong Cassidy Bar 20s and Hopalong Cassidy Ranch Toffees in 1954 to take advantage of Boyd's tour and Christmas. In September, the first time they made the candy bars, they sold 5591 boxes. In October, the first time they produced the toffees, they sold 2820 tins. In November, when Boyd was here, they sold 75 boxes and 3148 tins, and in December, with Boyd gone but Christmas here, they sold 91 and 10,306. After 1954, sales declined bit by bit along with interest in Hoppy.[158]

In 2012 and 2013, I asked the Master of Architecture students in my Popular Architecture and Design class at the University of Melbourne to design some Hopalong Cassidy products they might have produced to commemorate the Australian visit of William Boyd while reflecting on the fads and fashions of the day: things like the "Americanisation" of Australian popular culture, the popularity of Westerns, and playing cowboys and Indians, among others. Following is a tiny sample of what they made (Fig. 2.11).

Vegemite is a salty, tart, black spread eaten on toast, usually for breakfast. Australians love it, while foreigners regard it with deep suspicion. Did William Boyd sample Vegemite in Australia in 1954? Coincidently, the same year, Alan Weeks composed the catchy commercial jingle, "Happy Little Vegemites" (1954), which referred to the healthy dispositions of children who ate Vegemite.[159] Architecture student Craig Noyce redesigned the Vegemite label to include a picture of Hopalong Cassidy and declare consumers "Happy Little Hopalongs" instead of "Happy Little Vegemites."

Almost up there with Vegemite as a national favourite is Tim Tam chocolate biscuits (i.e., cookies), named after the American thoroughbred

2 HOPALONG CASSIDY ON TOUR   83

Fig. 2.11 (*Clockwise*) Hopalong Cassidy Vegemite, Tim Tams, sunscreen and boomerang

racehorse, Tim Tam (1955–1982), winner of the 1958 Kentucky Derby. Architecture student Nathalie Sanchez thought that any biscuit named after a horse would appeal to Hopalong Cassidy, so she put his picture on the packet and changed the shape of the biscuits from oblong to Hoppy riding Topper.

Australians have one of the highest rates of skin cancer in the world. Architecture student Tom Eckersley chose sunscreen for his product because he thought someone as public-minded as Hopalong Cassidy would want people to be "sun smart." He selected a trigger mechanism over a roll-on ball or pressure pack to associate it with the gun-toting cowboy.

They sold tens of thousands of Hopalong Cassidy toy pistols and holsters in Australia during the 1950s. Architecture student Xiao Wang noted the similarity in the shape of a gun and a boomerang and produced a Hopalong Cassidy boomerang and holster. William Boyd was shown how to throw a boomerang on at least two occasions and received several boomerangs as gifts from his Australian fans. A boomerang was not only a unique Australian souvenir, but it also expressed the hope that the person who received it would return to Australia. Alas, Boyd rode into the sunset, never to return.

So Long, Pardner

It is not surprising that William Boyd attracted such huge crowds in Melbourne and the other Australian capital cities he visited in 1954. His trip coincided with a worldwide fascination with the American Wild West, which included children playing cowboys and Indians, and suburban adults living in ranch houses, wearing Western-style shirts and jeans, barbequing outdoors, and square dancing. Furthermore, during Australia's drab post-war years, before Melbourne hosted the Olympic Games and got television in 1956, the population was eager for cheap thrills and glamour in their daily lives, which Boyd's visit delivered in spades. As an outsider and a celebrity in Australia for a short time, he was able to open doors closed to others and look at things with fresh eyes. For example, while raising money for local "crippled" children, Boyd probably met more blind, deaf, and disabled people in 16 days than most did in a lifetime. He also put disability on the front-page decades before people recognised it was an important issue (the International Year of Disabled Persons didn't happen until 1981—27 years after his visit).

Most people welcomed Boyd to Australia in 1954, but some—both from the far left and the far right—were cynical about his reasons for coming. 'The selling point of the visit is alleged to be "raising funds for crippled children," a very laudable proposition but is it true?' Rex Chiplin wrote in the Australian Communist Party newspaper, *The Tribune*. 'Stores are full of Hopalong cowboy suits and guns; they're selling like hot cakes because, by an extraordinary coincidence, Boyd's visit is on the eve of the Christmas shopping spree.'[160] Likewise, W. Sinclair, a Texas-born fire and brimstone Christian from Bouldercombe, Queensland, said: 'Hopalong Cassidy is the spearhead of a devilish scheme, not only to demoralise the rising generation in all English-speaking countries, but to capitalise in a big way on sales of cowboy suits, pistols, knives, and other paraphernalia of a supposed Wild West. [...] If Dad and Mum have to appeal to Cassidy to keep their kids in order, then woe be to Australia and all countries under the demonic spell.'[161]

Boyd never returned to Australia, despite promising he would. Such was the fickleness of children towards their screen idols in those days, Hopalong Cassidy's popularity nosedived after the release of the Walt Disney film *Davy Crockett, King of the Wild Frontier* (1955). He stopped appearing in public as Hoppy when his beloved horse Topper died in 1961. Boyd died from the effects of Parkinson's disease aged 77 in 1972. Channelling Bill Armbrust for fun, I wrote a short poem about their demise:

> Hoppy's horse, Topper,
> Was smart like its rider;
> Unlike California,
> Hoppy's off-sider.
> Topper showed Hoppy the way,
> Never leading him astray,
> And helping him to save the day.
> Hoppy stayed inside
> After Topper died,
> Heart-broken by the loss
> Of his faithful white horse.

Notes

1. Grace Bradley Boyd and Michael Cochran, *Hopalong Cassidy: An American Legend*, York, Pennsylvania: Gemstone Publishing Inc., 2008, pp. 325–327.
2. 'Darwin Says: Howdy, Hoppy ... and It Sure Was A Welcome,' *The Sun News-Pictorial* (Victoria), 10 November 1954, p. 3.
3. 'Darwin is Angry with Tired Hoppy,' *The News* (South Australia), 10 November 1954, p. 31.

4. 'Darwin Says: Howdy, Hoppy ... and It Sure Was A Welcome.'
5. 'Hundreds Greet Hopalong ...,' *The Northern Territory News* (Northern Territory) 11 November 1954, p. 1.
6. 'Darwin Says: Howdy, Hoppy ... and It Sure Was A Welcome.'
7. 'Hero-Worshipping, etc.,' *The Northern Territory News*, 11 November 1954, p. 1.
8. Ibid.
9. 'Darwin is Angry with Tired Hoppy.'
10. 'Hundreds Greet Hopalong ....'
11. 'Darwin Says: Howdy, Hoppy ... and It Sure Was a Welcome.'
12. Eric Jolliffe, 'Hopalong, He Bin Proper Hero There,' *The Sun-Herald* (New South Wales), 21 November 1954, p. 50.
13. Ibid.
14. 'Hundreds Greet Hopalong ....'
15. Monica Tan, 'Ernie Dingo and Richard Walley on the 40th Year of Their Welcome to Country,' *The Guardian* (Australia), https://www.theguardian.com/australia-news/2016/feb/23/ernie-dingo-and-richard-walley-on-the-40th-year-of-their-welcome-to-country, accessed 30 May 2022.
16. 'Good Luck Medals to be Unloaded,' *The Advertiser* (South Australia), 11 November 1954, p. 3.
17. J.A. Alexander (ed.), *Who's Who in Australia 1965*, Melbourne: Colorgravure Publications, 1965, p. 551.
18. Michael Bialoguski, *The Petrov Story*, William Heinemann Ltd, Melbourne, 1955.
19. Ibid, p. 222.
20. Ibid, p. 225.
21. 'Leydin to be Nauru Administrator. Promote Man Who Met Mrs. Petrov,' *The Courier-Mail* (Queensland), 29 April 1954, p. 1.
22. 'Darwin Excited. Pupils Rave Over Hoppy,' *The Courier-Mail* 11 November 1954, p. 6.
23. 'Darwin is Angry with Tired Hoppy.'
24. Ibid.
25. 'Hundreds greet Hopalong ....'
26. Ibid.
27. Thanks to Peter Dunham of Anula, Northern Territory, for 'The Coming of Cassidy' by Bill Armbrust.
28. 'Hopalong Cassidy in Darwin,' *The Newcastle Morning Herald and Miners' Advocate* (New South Wales), 11 November 1954, p.8.
29. 'Darwin is Angry with Tired Hoppy.'
30. 'Hundreds Greet Hopalong ....'

31. G.J. Aitken, Letter to William Boyd, 22 October 1954, William Boyd Collection at the American Heritage Centre University of Wyoming, Laramie, USA.
32. 'Hundreds Greet Hopalong ....'
33. Eric Jolliffe.
34. Ibid.
35. Ted Egan, Telephone interview with Derham Groves, 2013.
36. Geoff James, Email to Derham Groves, 16 August 2013.
37. John Waters, Email to Derham Groves, 19 August 2013. He said the car was a Ford Customline.
38. Vic Streatham, Telephone interview with Groves, 2013. He said it was a Land Rover.
39. 'Hopalong Cassidy in Australia,' *The Morning Bulletin* (Queensland), 11 November 1954, p. 4.
40. Terence Cody, Email to Derham Groves, 28 July 2013.
41. Phynea Paspalis, Telephone interview with Derham Groves, 2014.
42. Arthur Que Noy, Telephone interview with Derham Groves, 2013.
43. 'Hundreds greet Hopalong ....'
44. 'Native Captured First Jap Here,' *The News*, 26 July 1945, p. 4.
45. 'Portland Rotary,' *The Portland Guardian* (Victoria), 17 September 1942, p. 2.
46. Ted Egan, Email to Derham Groves, 14 September 2013.
47. Ibid.
48. Ted Egan, 2013.
49. Grace Bradley Boyd and Michael Cochran, p. 272.
50. Tom Jones, 'William Boyd aka Hopalong Cassidy,' *Tom Jones Interviews for 3UZ Radio: The Actors*, Lyric, 2013.
51. Vic Streatham.
52. John Waters.
53. Ernie Chin, Email to Derham Groves, 6 December 2013.
54. Geoff James.
55. John Waters.
56. Greg Tonks, Telephone interview with Derham Groves, 2013.
57. 'Darwin Excited. Pupils Rave Over Hoppy.'
58. Dr. Bill Day, 'Aboriginal People of Darwin: The Bagot Community,' https://www.drbilldayanthropologist.com/resources/Bagot%20 Aboriginal%20Community%202012.pdf, accessed 3 January 2017.
59. 'Hoppy Thrills Darwin Schoolchildren,' *The Advertiser*, 11 November 1954, p. 3.
60. Don White, Interview with Derham Groves, 2014.
61. Eric Jolliffe.
62. Grace Bradley Boyd and Michael Cochran, pp. 325–326.

63. Don White.
64. Eric Jolliffe.
65. 'Star Pictures,' *The Northern Territory News*, 4 November 1954, p. 7.
66. Eric Jolliffe.
67. Gayne Dexter, 'Limelight,' *The Sun-Herald*, 25 April 1954, p. 49.
68. Peter Golding, 'Hopalong Got Him Hopping,' *The Argus* (Victoria), 19 May 1954, p. 3.
69. Anne Bradley, 'She Married Adventure. Elsa Chauvel: Her Husband's "Man Friday,"' *The Australian Women's Weekly* (Australia), 7 August 1957, p. 7.
70. Douglas Lockwood, 'Whar's Clancy? He Can Only Find Hopalong,' *The Mail*, 22 August 1953, p. 9.
71. Keith Dunstan, 'Day by Day,' *The Courier-Mail*, 21 May 1954, p. 1.
72. Douglas Lockwood.
73. Dan Grayson, Letter to Alex Tolmer, 6 July 1954, William Boyd Collection.
74. Ibid.
75. Ibid.
76. Grace Bradley Boyd and Michael Cochran, p. 326.
77. Tom Farrell, 'The Pied Piper of Hollywood,' *The Daily Telegraph* (New South Wales), 13 November 1954, p. 7.
78. 'Proposed Itinerary, William Boyd tour of Australia—1954,' William Boyd Collection.
79. Ibid.
80. J. Altham *The Deaf Children's Chronicle* (Victoria), 1 December 1954, p. 5.
81. Ken Wise, Telephone interview with Derham Groves, 2013.
82. 'Tonic for Small Patients. Hoppy Blazes Happy Trail in Hospital,' *The Daily Mirror* (New South Wales), 13 November 1954, n.p.
83. Silvana Cattapan, Telephone interview with Derham Groves, 2013.
84. 'Hospital Agog as Hopalong Pulls His Six-Shooters,' *The Herald*, 12 November 1954, p. 5.
85. Wendy Secombe, Email to Derham Groves, 11 July 2013.
86. 'Doggone, A Stampede. Hold It Pard,' *The Sun News-Pictorial*, 13 November 1954, p. 19.
87. 'Hospital Agog as Hopalong Pulls His Six-Shooters.'
88. 'Hoppy's on the Trail,' *The Sun* (New South Wales), 13 November 1954, p. 3.
89. Allan Rouse, Telephone interview with Derham Groves, 2013.
90. 'Six-gun King Rode Into Their Hearts,' *The Sun News-Pictorial*, 13 November 1954, p. 3.
91. Paul Haar, Email to Derham Groves, 15 June 2013.

92. 'Tonic for Small Patients. Hoppy Blazes Happy Trail in Hospital.'
93. 'Hopalong Cassidy—and the Kids,' *Pix*, 27 November 1954, p. 25.
94. Mrs. D. Wheeler, Telephone interview with Derham Groves, 2013.
95. William Ellis Green, 'WEG's Weekend,' 13 November 1954, p. 4.
96. 'Proposed Itinerary, William Boyd tour of Australia—1954.'
97. 'Hoppy's on the Trail.'
98. Margaret Cooper, Email to Derham Groves, 24 August 2013.
99. 'Equestrian Olympics to Stockholm,' *The Cairns Post* (Queensland), 14 May 1954, p. 1.
100. Ben Lewin, Email to Derham Groves, 1 November 2012.
101. Peter Freckleton, Email to Derham Groves, 16 July 2013.
102. Norman Marshall, *The Yooralla Story 1918-1977*, Melbourne: Yooralla Society of Victoria, 1976, p. 84.
103. 'Proposed Itinerary, William Boyd tour of Australia—1954.'
104. 'Hospital Agog as Hopalong Pulls His Six-Shooters.'
105. 'Susan Just Knew it was Hopalong,' *The Argus*, 13 November 1954, p. 3.
106. Ibid.
107. 'Hospital Agog as Hopalong Pulls His Six-Shooters.'
108. 'Hoppy's Visit was a "Fairy Tale" Come True,' *The Herald*, 15 November 1954, p. 3.
109. Janice Nixon, *The Deaf Children's Chronicle*, 1 December 1954, p. 6.
110. Emerald A. Goetze (comp.), *Publicity Book for 'Hopalong Cassidy Visit' to Melbourne on Behalf of Children's Welfare Association of Victoria*, Melbourne, 1954, William Boyd Collection.
111. 'Susan Just Knew it was Hopalong.'
112. 'Proposed itinerary William Boyd tour of Australia—1954.'
113. 'This is a Hold-Up!' *The Listener In* (Victoria), 6-12 November 1954, p. 10.
114. 'Stadium Show for Hopalong,' *Listener In* 23–29 October 1954, p. 3.
115. 'Children Hurt in Rush to See Cowboy at Circus,' *The Age*, 13 November 1954, p. 1.
116. Lorraine Perry, Telephone interview with Derham Groves, 2013.
117. Leo St Leon, Telephone interview with Derham Groves, 2013.
118. 'Proposed itinerary William Boyd tour of Australia—1954.'
119. Robert Perry, Email to Derham Groves, 18 February 2014.
120. 'Children Hurt in Rush to See Cowboy at Circus.'
121. Lorraine Perry.
122. Trevor Parkes, Telephone interview with Derham Groves, 2013.
123. William Ellis Green.
124. 'Near Riot as 20,000 Crush Hoppy's Show,' *The Sun News-Pictorial*, 13 November 1954, p. 1.
125. Lorraine Perry.
126. Ray Johnson, Telephone interview with Derham Groves, 2013.

127. Ibid.
128. Tom Dumpleton, Telephone interview with Derham Groves, 2014.
129. Grace Bradley Boyd and Michael Cochran, pp. 293–294.
130. Grant Aldous, Telephone interview with Derham Groves, 2013.
131. St Leon (2013).
132. 'Children Hurt in Rush to See Cowboy at Circus.'
133. Terry Parkes.
134. Lorraine Perry.
135. 'Children Hurt in Rush to See Cowboy at Circus.'
136. Tom Dumpleton.
137. 'Children Hurt in Rush to See Cowboy at Circus.'
138. Lorraine Perry.
139. 'Children Hurt in Rush to See Cowboy at Circus.'
140. Tom Dumpleton.
141. 'Children Hurt in Rush to See Cowboy at Circus.'
142. Terry Guest, Telephone interview with Derham Groves, 2013.
143. Tom Jones.
144. 'Hoppy Fans in Wild Stampede,' *The Argus*, 13 November 1954, p. 1.
145. Harry L. Rinkler, *Hopalong Cassidy: King of the Cowboy Merchandisers* by Harry L. Rinker, Atglen, Pennsylvania: Schiffer Publishing Ltd, 1995.
146. Keith Harris & Co. Ltd file, William Boyd Collection.
147. Ibid.
148. W. Owen Pty Ltd, Advertising brochure, William Boyd Collection.
149. Quote from Hopalong Cassidy Game instructions in the author's collection.
150. Harry L. Rinkler, p. 24.
151. W. Owen Pty Ltd file, William Boyd Collection.
152. Ibid.
153. Fyna Foods Pty Ltd file, William Boyd Collection.
154. Ibid.
155. The Queensland Museum in Brisbane has a Hoppy Belt Pouch in its collection, https://collections.qm.qld.gov.au/objects/112095/belt-pouch-with-swap-card-and-toys, accessed 30 May 2022.
156. Hoppy swap card, series 1, no. 16, author's collection.
157. Hopalong Cassidy Ranch Toffee tin, author's collection.
158. Besters Sweets Pty Ltd file, William Boyd Collection.
159. "Happy Little Vegemites," https://www.youtube.com/watch?v=h5r3HAJh8es, accessed 30 May 2022.
160. Rex Chiplin, 'Rex Chiplin Says …,' *The Tribune* (New South Wales), 17 November 1954, p. 2.
161. W. Sinclair, 'Hopalong Cassidy,' *The Morning Bulletin* (Queensland), 17 November 1954, p. 5.

CHAPTER 3

Whiplash

Abstract This chapter is about *Whiplash*, the ATV Western TV series set and filmed in Australia in 1959–1960. It talks about its American star, Peter Graves, and his family's reactions to living in Australia. It discusses the impressive group of Hollywood screenwriters who wrote for the series, including Gene Roddenberry (*Star Trek*), Harry Julian Fink (*Dirty Harry*), and Don Ingalls (*Have Gun Will Travel*). It considers some problems *Whiplash*'s producers both faced and created while making the series, including wet weather, unsafe sets, and being micro-managed from London. It discusses the talented black and white Australian actors who performed in *Whiplash*, such as Anthony Wickert, Robert Tudawali, Chips Rafferty, and Annette Andre. It examines how the series presented Australia through a "Hollywood lens," especially its pioneering history and First Nations People. Finally, this chapter looks at the critics' reaction to *Whiplash*, which was mostly negative, although I argue unjustly so.

Keywords Aboriginals • Actors and actresses • Alice Springs • Artransa • Australia • Cobb & Co. • Peter Graves • Television

© The Author(s), under exclusive license to Springer Nature Switzerland AG 2022
D. Groves, *Australian Westerns in the Fifties*,
https://doi.org/10.1007/978-3-031-12883-7_3

The American Star

After appearing in several feature films, including *Rogue River* (1951), *Stalag 17* (1953), and *The Long Grey Line* (1955), the American actor Peter Graves (1926–2010)—real name Peter Aurness—played Jim Newton in five seasons of the American kids-and-horses Western TV series *Fury* (1955–1960), about the adventures of his adopted son Joey and a black stallion named Fury. A sixth season was in the offing, but Graves left to play Christopher "Chris" Cobb, the Boston-born founder of the legendary Australian stagecoach line Cobb & Co., in a new Western TV series set and filmed entirely in Australia called *Whiplash* (1960–1961). 'I did a lot of thinking before quitting [*Fury*],' he told *The Pensacola News Journal*. 'But I finally decided it would be best for me to leave. I'll be going to Australia in about ten days, and after I get settled, my wife and three children will follow. We plan to be there about a year, shooting 39 segments of the series.'[1] (In the end, they filmed only 34 episodes.)

As an American in nineteenth-century Australia, Graves' character Chris Cobb was able to see things differently with fresh eyes. While only a relative newcomer to Australia, he acquired superb bush skills that earned him the respect and friendship of Australia's oldest inhabitants—the Aboriginals. And being on the road, he was able to travel widely and meet all kinds of people. According to *The Arizona Daily Sun*, Cobb was 'comparable to Davy Crockett and Jim Bowie in that he actually became a legend in his own lifetime.'[2] Although in my view, Cobb and his offsider Dan Ledward (Anthony Wickert) were more like Todd Stiles (Martin Milner, 1931–2015) and Buz Murdoch (George Maharis, b.1928) in the American TV series *Route 66* (1960–1964), who sought adventure cruising Australian instead of American roads in a stagecoach rather than a Corvette.

The model for Chris Cobb was Freeman Cobb (1830–1878), the real-life American businessman who came to Australia in 1853 and founded the stagecoach line Cobb & Co. (1853–1924) (Fig. 3.1).[3] Its coaches travelled 28,000 miles per week and used 6000 horses per day.[4] The producers of *Whiplash* had understandably wanted to name the series "Cobb & Co."[5] and its leading man "Freeman Cobb."[6] However, a rival production company had beaten them to it: The NTA Film Network (1956–1961) had already bought the rights to those names for a Western TV series it was planning to make in Australia but never did.[7] It did not matter since Chris Cobb owed as much to artifice as he did to history. For example, he

3 WHIPLASH   93

Fig. 3.1 Freeman Cobb (*left*) and Peter Graves as Chris Cobb

wore a pull-on long-sleeve shirt with a lace-up V-neck collar that looked more like something a 1950s folk singer might have worn than an 1850s bushman—not to mention his slouch hat that did not look quite right either. 'I asked Mr. Fox [*Whiplash*'s American producer] about the hat,' Nan Musgrove of *The Australian Women's Weekly* said.

> He said frankly it was a liberty—that the motif of *Whiplash* was Australian and that the Digger hat was loved overseas as a symbol of Australians. Chris Cobb, therefore, wears a hat that I'm sure no Digger would recognise as his. I am carping, but I think many Australians will carp at things like this that occur throughout the series and be puzzled at the fact that Cobb & Co. were ever dragged into the series.[8]

Graves and Ben Fox were adamant that Cobb was less violent than other Western TV heroes. 'I don't wear a gun-belt, for instance,' Graves told Bill Olsen of *The Sydney Morning Herald*. 'When I have to use a pistol, I stick it in my belt. But don't get the idea there's no action—there's plenty, but we're trying to get away from that old Western stuff.'[9] Consequently, Cobb sometimes used a boomerang, which Fox was at pains to stress was 'a blunt boomerang. He can only knock out an opponent, not kill him. [*Whiplash*] is a strictly non-violent production. The public is sick of violence.'[10] But Fox forgot to tell Gene Roddenberry (1921–1991) because in "Episode in Bathurst" (1961), written by him,

Cobb kills a man with a boomerang: Cobb investigates the Denvers brothers—Matt (Joe McCormick), Tiny (Chuck Faulkner, 1922–2000), and Pecos (Richard Meikle, 1929–1991). The three Texas gunslingers have erected a barbed-wire toll gate outside Bathurst, 200 kilometres west of Sydney, to extort money from travellers, including Cobb & Co. The locals want Cobb to shoot the troublemakers. However, he argues it would be ugly, stupid, and vicious and might even catch on. So, when Tiny tries to gun down Cobb after receiving a walloping from him in a barroom fistfight, Cobb grabs a boomerang instead of a gun and throws it at Tiny. It hits him on the head, killing him stone dead. 'If I seem a bit out of breath, I can tell you that running around in this heat playing the part of "baddie," Tiny Denvers of the "Denvers Gang," [...] is no joke,'[11] Faulkner said. The next day, Cobb and Matt face off in a shootout. This time he uses a stockwhip instead of a boomerang to defend himself—anything but a gun! Cobb first disarms Matt, then "whip-dances" him and Pecos out of town. 'Peter did learn how to crack that whip and wrap it around me,'[12] Graves's wife, Joan Endress (m.1950–2010), told me in 2020. She still had Cobb's whip and hat on display in the den of her Los Angeles home (Fig. 3.2).

In 1960, the American entertainment industry announced that it wanted to reduce violence on the screen.[13] Graves' response was *not* to call *Whiplash* a Western. 'We're trying to keep away from the word "Western" by labelling the series a romantic adventure,'[14] he said. Similarly, Fox 'was quick to correct the impression that *Whiplash* is "an Australian Western,"' *The Age* said, because 'it has a refreshingly different background, and there is a definite emphasis on character in action.'[15] Having compared *Whiplash* to *Route 66* earlier, I understand what they meant. But if it looks like a duck, swims like a duck, and quacks like a duck, then it probably is a duck. *Whiplash* had all of the signs of being a Western, including a typical Western theme song. "Whiplash" (1960) was sung by the British-Australian country-and-western singer Frank Ifield (b.1937) and written by the British composer Edwin Astley (1922–1998), also responsible for the TV theme songs of *The Adventures of Robin Hood* (1955–1960), *The Buccaneers* (1956–1957), and *Ivanhoe* (1958–1959). As the sound of a cracking whip punctuates "Whiplash," it reminded Nan Musgrove of "Mule Train" (1949) and "Rawhide" (1958),[16] although it was neither the "earworm" nor as popular as them. As was common in those days, the lyrics quickly established what the TV series was about:

Fig. 3.2 Chris Cobb and his stockwhip from *Whiplash Painting Book* (n.d.)

Whiplash, whiplash,
Whiplash, whiplash,
In 1851,
The great Australian gold rush,
The only law a gun,
The only shelter wild bush,
Whiplash, whiplash,
Umm-mm, umm-mm.

Through mulga wood and desert,
The stage thunders by,
Through Sydney to Camden,

And on to Gundagai,
Whiplash, whiplash,
Whiplash, whiplash,
Umm-mm, umm-mm.[17]

Despite the denials, most people regarded *Whiplash* as a Western. After all, "a rose by any other name would smell as sweet." Thus, TV critics variously described it as 'a new Western—from Australia,'[18] 'Australia's own Western,'[19] the 'first Australian Western,'[20] a 'made-in-Australia TV Western,'[21] a Western [with] an Aussie flavour,'[22] and so on.

Clearly, it made sense for an American actor to play an American character in *Whiplash*.[23] However, there were other reasons for hiring Graves as well. 'When you see the Australian TV series *Whiplash* you will detect a decided American or semi-American accent,' warned *The Sydney Morning Herald* columnist "Granny," aka Sydney Deamer (1891–1962). 'The reason, I'm told, is that films of this type cost so much to make that an eye must always be kept on the American market—and Americans don't hear enough of our accent to understand us.'[24] He was certainly correct about Americans having trouble with Australian accents. 'Casting for the series was difficult because the Australian accent, particularly in women, was grating on American ears,' *Whiplash*'s American associate producer John Meredyth Lucas (1919–2002) said. 'We settled, finally, on radio actors. They were used to playing with a number of accents. We had them use English North Country. It sounds foreign but easily recognizable to American ears and lacks the harshness of the Australian product.'[25] Deamer was also right about the high cost of the series. Australian TV shows made for local audiences cost nothing like the £650,000 that it took to make *Whiplash*.[26]

Australian television had been going for only three years in 1959 (20 years less than in America), which was another reason for having an experienced TV actor like Peter Graves in *Whiplash*. Many Australian actors were unfamiliar with the "new" medium. Take the Sydney actor Anthony Wickert, for example, who played Cobb & Co.'s top stagecoach driver Dan Ledward in 26 episodes. While he had acted in plays and films, he had no television experience. 'Peter and I became good friends,' Wickert said. 'I worked with him almost every day, and I learned a lot about making those kinds of programmes from him because he had been in two or three TV series before that in America. Peter was a good "tutor,"'[27] he said. The Australian actress Annette Andre (b.1939) made three episodes of

Whiplash—"Episode in Bathurst," "Storm River" (1961), and "Dark Runs the Sea" (1961). She also learned a lot working with Graves on the series. He 'was such a lovely man,' Andre said. 'And very helpful to us because he was a very experienced American actor. He was one of the few at the time that we could learn from. Sometimes there were problems on set with the odd argument or disagreement or upset or just nerves, but Peter always calmed things down.'[28]

Another reason for having an American star of *Whiplash* was because Australians were in awe of American popular culture. The Australian architect Robin Boyd (1919–1971) even coined the term "Austerica" to describe it: 'Austerica thrives in the matted fringe of the entertainment business, as in the fake American accents on the radio and television, the crew-cuts in the Australian magazine illustrations laboriously plagiarised from American journals, and all the muddled Americana of the clothing fashion world,' he wrote in his scathing critique of Australia's suburbs, *The Australian Ugliness* (1960). 'Advertisements of all kinds, displays, window dressing—all the visual trivia of modern Australia—is dominated by the Austerican outlook, for Austerica's credo is that everything desirable, exciting, luxurious and enviable in the twentieth century is American.'[29] Consequently, any Australian TV show worth its salt in those days 'had to have an OS star, even a third-rater,'[30] explained Andy, a character in *The Silent Country* (2009) by the Australian novelist Di Morrissey (b.1943), which mentions *Whiplash* in passing. According to him:

> Producers wouldn't use our top-notch talent. Didn't think that they would have the drawing power. But they learned, eventually [...]. Have you heard of Peter Graves? He came out to do an Australian "Western" and went back to star in the original *Mission Impossible* TV series [...]. I'm told that [... he] was a nice man but those *Whiplash* scripts he had to work with were abysmal.[31]

THE GRAVESES IN AUSTRALIA

Peter Graves arrived in Sydney on 1 October 1959 to start work on *Whiplash*.[32] Coming to Australia was a double-edged sword for him. He had reluctantly turned down playing opposite the American actress, dancer, and singer Ginger Rogers (1911–1995) in the American stage production of the musical *Pink Jungle* (1959).[33] (His place was taken by Leif Erickson, 1911–1986.) On the other hand, Graves fortuitously 'missed the actors' strike which took place in his absence,' Joe Finnigan of *The Anderson Herald* said. 'Thousands of Hollywood actors were out of work, but Pete wasn't affected,'[34] because he was in Australia making *Whiplash*.

Graves was already quite well known in Australia because of *Fury*.[35] Many people also knew that he was the younger brother of the American actor James Arness (1923–2011), who played Matt Dillon in the popular American Western series *Gunsmoke* (1955–1975).[36] 'He's terribly interested in Australia,' Graves told Nan Musgrove, who had asked him whether he also might come to Australia. 'He makes quite a number of personal-appearance tours. Jim's a tremendous man, [...] shoulders that wide and much taller than me. He's a good actor, too. *Gunsmoke* made him that way.'[37] In 1961, WTVT in Florida showed *Gunsmoke* at 7:30 p.m. on Tuesday nights followed by *Whiplash* at 8:00 p.m. Therefore, 'the two brothers face peril and adventure half a world apart, yet side-by-side,'[38] the *Tampa Bay Times* reported.

'Mrs. Graves, like her husband, worried over their decision to come [to Australia],' Musgrove said. 'She hopes [...] that their "Australian adventure" will be just right for Peter's career and the Graves family's future prosperity.'[39] But Joan Endress need not have worried about that, because Graves earned $200,000 a year for playing Chris Cobb,[40] plus a large percentage of *Whiplash*'s profits,[41] which amounted annually to nearly $1 million.[42] (The average wage for an American worker in 1959 was $5400 per year.[43]) Peter's agent was responsible for getting him such a good deal,[44] Endress said.

The Graveses were so confident that *Whiplash* would do well, they sold their house in Los Angeles before coming to Australia.[45] 'Ever since we were married, we've lived in a cosy place not far from the Pacific on the Western rim of Hollywood,' Graves told Musgrove. 'All this has to be changed now to a small place in a suburb on the outskirts of Sydney,'[46] he said, referring to the house he had just rented overlooking Bilgola Beach near Avalon Beach, 37 kilometres north of Sydney (Fig. 3.3). Endress and the Graveses' three daughters—Kelly (8), Claudia (5), and Amanda (1)—joined him there six weeks later. In those days, it took 17 hours to fly from Los Angeles to Sydney with stops at San Francisco, Honolulu, Canton Island, and Fiji. 'It took forever!' Joan recalled 60 years later. 'We were so exhausted by the time we reached Avalon Beach that we went straight to bed, only to be "eaten alive" by mosquitoes overnight.'[47] Later, the Graveses' neighbours also warned them about blowflies, snakes, and

Fig. 3.3   Houses and shops in Avalon Beach (c.1960)

spiders—which horrified Joan the most. But that still did not stop Kelly from catching big hairy ones and bringing them home in jars.[48]

Spiders also frightened John Meredyth Lucas. He had rented a house at Wahroonga, 18 kilometres northwest of Sydney, for his wife, the Australian actress Joan Winfield (1918–1978), and their three children, aged from two to seven.[49] 'As a foreigner, reading the horrifying posters the government put out for travellers and thinking of the children playing in the yard, I had the feeling that every misstep would be our last,' Lucas said. 'So I had the house and grounds fumigated before the family arrived.'[50] But all that did was flush the survivors into the house!

Having been uprooted from her school and friends in Los Angeles, eight-year-old Kelly Graves found living at Avalon Beach difficult. 'I was pretty young but old enough to realise that I was a fish out of water,' she said. 'They teased me at school because I had an accent, which, at age eight, was devastating for me. All of the schoolwork was different. They'd ask us to add up pounds, shillings, and pence, but I didn't know how to do it. And people didn't know how to relate to me. I was the girl from Hollywood whose father was an actor. People would stare and point at me. The whole time in Australia, I felt like Alice down the rabbit hole. Everything was inside out and upside down.'[51] On the other hand, Kelly's mother Joan Endress enjoyed living there. 'It was an adventure,' she said. 'We were young—I was 30 or something like that—so we just did it and loved it. Everybody was so wonderful. They couldn't have been more helpful. We met lots of people and made lots of friends over there. I wish it had lasted longer, and so did Peter, but what will be will be. It was the start of a lifelong love affair with Australia, because we went back again almost every other year.'[52]

Regardless of whether you liked living there or not, Avalon Beach was nothing like Los Angeles. Kelly thought it was like 'an old west town ... something out of a Western TV show. The shops had wooden sidewalks. The school had just a dirt playground. It was completely different to what we had in Los Angeles.'[53] Kelly's memories of Avalon Beach's architecture were "wayward," according to long-time resident Geoff Searl.[54] However, I suspect the impression it left on her as an eight-year-old is more significant than what it was like, especially as she was living there only because her father was making a Western TV series in Australia. In any case, Avalon Beach did not have many mod-cons in 1959–1960. 'In those days, there weren't any supermarkets like we had back home,' Joan recalled. 'So, I had to get used to going to the greengrocer, the butcher, and the baker all separately. There was no aluminium. No plastic. And no cranberry sauce for Thanksgiving Dinner!'[55]

The Graveses returned to Los Angeles in October 1960 after *Whiplash* was finished. 'We pioneered something,'[56] Peter declared. Nevertheless, he was glad to be home. 'After a year with kangaroos, koala bears, aborigines, and technical difficulties, Graves is happy to return to Hollywood for good,' Charles Witbeck of *The Record* said. 'At times out there, Hollywood seemed like a misty town and that I'd been away for ten years,' Graves said. 'I know now where I belong.'[57] The money he had earned from *Whiplash* enabled them to buy a nicer house in Los Angeles than the one they sold before leaving for Australia. Peter lived there for the rest of his life, and Joan still lives there.

Graves took a while to find "the next big thing" following *Whiplash*. He made a pilot for a private detective TV series called *Las Vegas Beat* (1961) for NBC,[58] which did not progress beyond that. He appeared in *The Captains and the Kings* (1962), a play about the US Navy's first atomic submarine by the American playwright Leo Lieberman (1916–2000). 'I've never done a Broadway role, and I need the experience,'[59] Graves said. He also made a pilot for a ship-at-sea TV series called *Mr. Kingston* (1964) for ABC. 'The good thing about this show is that the captain [played by the American actor Walter Pigeon (1897–1984)] and

"Mr. Kingston" [the first mate, played by Graves] are naturally enmeshed in everything that goes on aboard the ship,' he said. 'You can get involved in all sorts of situations, drama, romance, comedy, and mystery.'[60] While it sounds like the hit 1970s TV series *The Love Boat* (1976–1990), *Mr. Kingston* did not progress beyond the pilot either. Graves was eventually cast in the American spy TV series *Mission Impossible* (1966–1973) as secret agent Jim Phelps—the role for which he is best remembered.

THE WRITERS

Whiplash was created by the New Zealand-born Australian screenwriter Michael Noonan (1921–2000)[61] and the Australian screenwriter Michael Plant (1930–1965) (Fig. 3.4). Noonan moved to London in 1957, returning frequently to Australia for work.[62] He created *The Flying Doctor* (1959), a drama TV series about Australia's famous Royal Flying Doctor Service (RFDS), starring the American actor Richard Denning (1914–1998) as Dr. Greg Graham. It was produced by the Associated British Picture Corporation (1927–1970) and filmed in black-and-white mostly in England but also in Australia. Between 1961 and 1969, Noonan also wrote six children's books about the RFDS. Another drama TV series he created was *Riptide* (1969), about the adventures of charter boat skipper Moss Andrews played by the American actor Ty Hardin (1930–2017),

Fig. 3.4 Michael Plant (*left*) and Michael Noonan

who played Bronco Layne in the American Western TV series *Bronco* (1958–1962). *Riptide* was produced by ITV and filmed in colour in Sydney and the Great Barrier Reef off the coast of Queensland. It is worth noting that *Whiplash*, *The Flying Doctor*, and *Riptide* were all set in Australia and starred American actors.

Michael Plant began his career working as an actor, writer, and producer for the American-born Sydney radio producer, Grace Gibson (1905–1989). In 1940, she co-founded the radio production company Artransa (short for "American Transcription Radio Services Australia"). The company later moved into television production as well. While Gibson no longer had a stake in Artransa when *Whiplash* was filmed there, on 9 September 1960, she and her husband Ronnie Parr (d.1985) hosted a 'gay party at their home' attended by Peter Graves and others from the cast of *Whiplash*.[63] Plant moved to England in 1951 and then to America in 1955 where he did a course on television at the University of California. He also worked on several American TV dramas, including *Bourbon Street Beat* (1959–1960), *The Barbara Stanwyck Show* (1960–1961), and *The Detectives* (1959–1961). Plant had just purchased the Santa Monica home of the Mexican-American actress Delores del Rio (1904–1983) when *Whiplash* brought him back to Australia. 'I don't want to sound disloyal, but I have been away so long now I feel very un-Australian,'[64] he said upon his return.

I suspect that *Whiplash* was influenced by the American TV Western *Tales of Wells Fargo* (1957–1962), as the similarities are plain to see. Their respective heroes, Chris Cobb and Jim Hardie (Dale Robertson, 1923–2013), were based on real people: Cobb on Freeman Cobb, as mentioned, and Hardie on Fred J. Dodge (1854–1938), an undercover detective who worked for the American stagecoach line Wells Fargo. Cobb and Hardie were both adventurous, good-looking, resourceful, well-mannered, and so on. Also, the dangerous nature of driving a stagecoach placed them in identical risky situations. Indeed, John Meredyth Lucas described Cobb & Co. as 'the Wells Fargo of Australia. They had the same problems there as we had here in the old west. The only difference is the colour of the Indians. Cobb's wagons were attacked by aborigines who tossed boomerangs.'[65] Similarly, Charles Witbeck described *Whiplash* as 'an Aussie *Wells Fargo*-type show [… with Graves] taking pot-shots at bad guys or aborigines from a mail coach in somewhat the same manner as Dale Robertson chases gunmen on Monday nights.'[66]

If *Whiplash*'s concept was not brand new, then its locations and interactions with First Nations Australians were, which was why they made the series in the first place. 'Nearly all the American Westerns are shot within 30 miles of Hollywood, and a lot of that scenery is becoming mighty familiar to TV viewers,'[67] Peter Graves said. Therefore, 'the reason for travelling all the way to Australia to film a Western series—instead of shooting in the San Fernando Valley—involves financing plus the chance to show fans new backgrounds and real aborigines instead of the fake Hollywood extras who pose as Indians.'[68] Graves believed the screenwriters would benefit too because 'that country is so different from what we have here, it will be a distinctive peg to hang a story on.'[69] Also, *Whiplash*'s American producer, Maury Geraghty (1908–1987), felt that 'the Australian landscape [...] will help to sell the series overseas.'[70]

Surprisingly few Australian screenwriters wrote for *Whiplash*. One was James Clavell (1921–1994), best known for writing the screenplays for the blockbuster films *The Great Escape* (1963) and *To Sir with Love* (1967), and also the best-selling novels *King Rat* (1962) and *Tai-Pan* (1966), who lived in England. He wrote one episode of *Whiplash*, "Love Story in Gold" (1961). Another was Morris West (1916–1999), best known for writing the best-selling novels, *The Devil's Advocate* (1959) and *The Shoes of the Fisherman* (1963). He also wrote one episode, "The Hunters" (1961). A third was Ralph W. Peterson (1921–1996), best known for creating the popular Australian TV sitcom, *My Name's McGooley, What's Yours?* (1966–1968). He wrote six episodes, "A Dilemma in Wool" (1961), "Ribbons and Wheels" (1961), "Stage Fright" (1961), "The Adelaide Arabs" (1961), "The Canoomba Affair" (1961), and "The Magic Wire" (1961).

Most of the series' screenwriters came from Hollywood. Don Ingalls (1918–2014) wrote for many American TV series, including several popular Westerns, especially *Have Gun Will Travel* (1957–1963). Initially, he was *Whiplash*'s head writer. 'I was to function as a writer, re-writer, associate producer, be responsible for all story and script development (hustling for good writers), and coordinate between London, Hollywood, and Sydney!'[71] he told Stephen Vagg. However, things did not go well for Ingalls, as I shall explain later, and he ended up writing only four episodes, "The Secret of the Screaming Hills" (1961), "Storm River" (1961), "The Day of the Hunter" (1961), and "Solid Gold Brigade" (1961). Other Hollywood screenwriters who wrote for *Whiplash* included Ron Bishop (1921–1988), Gerry Day (1922–2013), David Evans (1893–1968), Daphne Field (the series' only female screenwriter), Harry Julian Fink (1923–2001), Richard Grey, Terence Maples (1915–1980), Oscar Millard

(1908–1990), Dwight Newton (1916–2013), Gene Roddenberry, Wells Root (1900–1993), and William Templeton (1913–1973). Collectively, they wrote for some of the most popular TV Westerns of the day, including *The Lone Ranger* (1949–1957), *Cheyenne* (1955–1963), *The Restless Gun* (1957–1959), *Tombstone Territory* (1957–1960), *Maverick* (1957–1962), *Tales of Wells Fargo*, *Wagon Train* (1957–1965), *Bat Masterson* (1958–1961), *Laramie* (1959–1963), and *Bonanza* (1959–1973). Two names stand out, though—Harry Julian Fink and Gene Roddenberry. Fink wrote 18 episodes of *Have Gun Will Travel*, but he is best known for writing the action thriller *Dirty Harry* (1971), starring Clint Eastwood (b.1930) who played Rowdy Yates in *Rawhide* (1959–1965). Fink wrote two episodes of *Whiplash*, "Rider on the Hill" (1961) and "Barbed Wire" (1961). Roddenberry wrote 24 episodes of *Have Gun Will Travel*, including "Helen of Abajinian" (1957), which won the Writers' Guild of America Award in 1958. But he is best known for creating the sci-fi TV series *Star Trek* (1966–1969), which was inspired by *Wagon Train*.[72] Roddenberry wrote four episodes of *Whiplash*, "Episode in Bathurst," "Dutchman's Reef" (1961), "Sarong" (1961), and "The Actress" (1961). He probably got involved because of his friendships with Ingalls[73] and Peter Graves.[74]

A lack of local knowledge sometimes got American screenwriters in trouble. For example, in "Act of Courage" (1961) by Gerry Day, teenager Mike McKenna (Brett Hart) keeps a koala that has the run of the house. 'Never underestimate the power and influence of that cuddly little koala,'[75] Ben Fox declared, wishing to capitalise on the American fascination with native Australian animals. However, koalas are not as cuddly as they appear, and the idea of having one as a pet was naïve and implausible as far as most Australian viewers were concerned (Fig. 3.5).

In Di Morrissey's novel *The Silent Country*, mentioned earlier, "Alec" blamed gaffes like this on the fact that *Whiplash*'s scripts were 'written by Yanks who'd never been here. Someone told me that one [...] called for a herd of ferocious killer sheep!'[76] I have heard this story used against the series,[77] although I suspect it is apocryphal because unlike koalas, Americans have sheep and know how they behave. On the other hand, there might be some truth in the story because Morrissey's mother, the TV producer Kay Roberts (1921–2008), worked at Artransa when they were making *Whiplash* there and might have heard something about the 'ferocious killer sheep.'[78] In either case, any problems with the scripts were usually sorted out on the set, as Anthony Wickert explained:

Fig. 3.5 Peter Graves as Chris Cobb with a koala

We would get a new script about every ten days. They were often carelessly researched and needed a lot of remedial work by either the script department, the director, or the actors. Sometimes I would read through my part and say, 'God, this is terrible! Do I have to say that?' Fortunately, Peter Graves was good because he knew how to turn poor dialogue into what people say.[79]

THE PRODUCERS

The American businessman Jack Wrather (1918–1984) and the British broadcaster Lew Grade (1906–1998) jointly backed *Whiplash*. Wrather owned the Disneyland Hotel in Anaheim, California, and also produced two popular American TV series, *Lassie* (1954–1974) and *The Lone Ranger*. Grade owned the British television broadcasting company Associated Television (ATV), part of the British television network

Independent Television (ITV) and was also behind several popular British historical drama TV series, such as *The Adventures of Robin Hood*, *The Buccaneers*, and *William Tell* (1958–1959). 'Then Wrather sold his interest [in *Whiplash*] to the British half, and they sort of muddled their way through,'[80] Peter Graves lamented.

The first executive producer of *Whiplash* was the Australian filmmaker Ralph Smart (1908–2001). His film credits included writing and directing the Australian-made "Meat Pie Western," *Bitter Springs*, starring the Australian actor "Chips" Rafferty (who played Trooper Len in *Kangaroo*), which had advanced the idea of land rights for Aboriginals—an enlightened and radical idea for its day. As Smart had close ties with ATV and ITV, his television credits included directing 19 episodes of *The Adventures of Robin Hood* and producing 13 episodes of *The Buccaneers* and 25 episodes of *William Tell*.

Whiplash's first producer was the American filmmaker Maury Geraghty (Fig. 3.6). His film credits included producing eight detective mysteries featuring "The Falcon" (1942–1945) and writing the screenplay for a

Fig. 3.6 Bren Brown, Maury Geraghty, Ross Wood, and Bob Wright (*clockwise*)

boxing drama also titled *Whiplash* (1948). Geraghty also directed or wrote many American TV series, including *Bonanza, Buffalo Bill Jr.* (1955–1956), *Laramie, Lassie* (which may explain how he came to work on the TV series *Whiplash*, via Jack Wrather), *The Gene Autry Show* (1950–1955), and *The Virginian*. He arrived in Sydney on 8 August 1959 for a ten-day visit to discuss casting and locations for *Whiplash*.[81] A month later, he returned with his family to start work on the series.[82] The Geraghtys lived at Avalon Beach, like the Graveses. According to long-time resident Nina Gow, Geraghty's son Ricky went to Avalon Beach Primary School, 'and all of us girls were in love with him.'[83]

Whiplash's first director was the Hungarian-born British-Australian filmmaker Peter Maxwell (1921–2013), whose experience was exclusively in television. Like Smart, he also had close ties with ITV and ATV. Thus, Maxwell's television credits included directing 4 episodes of *The Adventures of Robin Hood*, 6 episodes of *The Buccaneers*, and 17 episodes of *William Tell*. He arrived in Australia on 4 November 1959—only three days before he started filming "The Solid Gold Brigade" by Don Ingalls,[84] the first episode of *Whiplash* to be filmed, but not the first one shown.

The wealth of knowledge and experience did not stop *Whiplash* from getting off to a slow start. Instead of making one episode per week,[85] they had made only four by the end of 1959.[86] Everyone blamed the wet weather—at least publicly. 'Rain so far has proved the biggest hindrance to the *Whiplash* film unit on location in New South Wales,'[87] *The Age* reported. A thunderstorm forced everyone to suddenly down their 'washing pans, stockwhips, picks, cameras, and lynching ropes'[88] and run for cover while they were filming "The Solid Gold Brigade," Bill Olson reported. 'Our main enemy was the weather. When it rained, it lasted for days—even weeks,'[89] Peter Graves said. It was no doubt wet that year.[90] However, rain was not *Whiplash*'s only problem. According to Don Ingalls, the delays were caused mainly by the series' meddlesome and nervous backers in England:

> London unexpectedly insisted that the dailies—each day's shot film—be air expressed to London for their approval and suggestions and airmailed back to Sydney for the recommended revisions! This on a three-day shooting schedule! By the time we got the film back, we were already one or two shoots down the road. Trying to get actors back for re-shooting and/or looping, quickly proved impossible.[91]

To make matters worse, on 23 December 1959, ATV suspended the production of *Whiplash* and sent its trouble-shooter, the American executive producer Leslie Harris, to Australia to review the series' operations.[92] His television credits included producing 91 episodes of the American World War II naval drama series *Navy Log* (1955–1958) for CBS and 26 episodes of the British Elizabethan naval drama series *Sir Frances Drake* (1961–1962) for the Independent Television Programme Company (ITP), also owned by Grade. Everyone denied reports that *Whiplash* was to be cancelled,[93] although its future did not look too rosy.

To avoid everything from shutting down completely, Graves suggested returning to Hollywood 'to film "interiors" for his *Whiplash* series.'[94] It did not happen, however, probably due to the confusion it would have caused, as well as the cost. It was extremely frustrating for everyone, especially Graves. 'It took three months of analysis and argument to get *Whiplash* under control, plus a completely new production staff,'[95] he said.

> The waiting and waiting began to get on my nerves. It took us well over a year to finish a series we should have completed in six months. On occasion, when I thought I'd blow my top, I'd phone my agent and several friends in Hollywood, blow a little steam and I'd soon feel better. I'd decide to endure it a while longer.[96]

The production of *Whiplash* finally resumed on 4 March 1960.[97] Due to the delay, Graves had the producers 'over a barrel [...] with the time limitations written into his contract,'[98] one Hollywood insider said. It might explain how Graves could propose 'taking a month off in mid-July to jet to London for the Edgar Allan Poe thriller, *The Masque of the Red Death*, then over to Hollywood and back to Sydney by jet.'[99] No doubt they were relieved when the plan fell through because his absence would have held up *Whiplash* even more.

The changes made to *Whiplash* by Leslie Harris included him taking over from Ralph Smart as the series' new executive producer and replacing Maury Geraghty with Ben Fox, a 44-year-old Boston-born Harvard-trained lawyer, as its new producer. His television credits included producing seven episodes of the American crime series *Code 3* (1957) for Hal Roach Studios. While there, Fox met the versatile and more experienced filmmaker John Meredyth Lucas,[100] and invited him to become *Whiplash*'s associate producer and share the directing duties with Peter Maxwell. Of the 34 episodes released, Lucas directed 13, Maxwell 18, Fox 2, and

Geraghty 1. In Anthony Wickert's view, Lucas thought 'Australian history was a replica of American history,' and thus '*Whiplash* wasn't an Australian story, but an American story set in Australia.'[101] Annette Andre did not enjoy working with Lucas much either because he was 'a bit difficult. He wasn't easy to get on with,'[102] she said.

Whiplash's head writer Don Ingalls also lost his job in the "purge," although he was philosophical about it. While mourning his "dead" scripts, he had to acknowledge that the shooting schedule fell behind, post-production was a disaster, the budget went ballistic, and people had their egos bruised.[103] In the 1980s, Ingalls and Graves 'shared a good laugh about our Australian adventure—but in a loving way! Australia's movie-making industry has come a long way since then,'[104] Ingalls said. Other changes to *Whiplash*'s crew included replacing the sound recordist Don Connolly (b.1929) with Geoffrey Daniels, the music director Albert Elms (1920–2009) with Edwin Astley, the property master Jock Levy (1916–2016) with Frants Folmer, and the art director Peter Mullins (b.1931) with Charles Wolveridge (1903–1974), even though, in my opinion, he did an excellent job creating the series' Australian Wild West-style township, Fury Creek (more about it later).

It is worth noting that Mullins was married to the English actress Jennifer Jayne (1931–2006). 'When [the producers of *Whiplash*] heard that Peter was married to a television actress, they extended the invitation to me,'[105] she said. Jayne appeared in three of the first four episodes produced by Maury Geraghty, "The Actress," "The Solid Gold Brigade," and "Episode in Bathurst."[106] However, they cut her scenes from the latter two episodes and she did not appear in any others, even though there was a suggestion she had a recurring role in the series. It seems that when Mullins got the sack, Jayne was collateral damage. It might have even been the other way around, but I somehow doubt it. Either way, in November 1959, the Mullinses moved into a house at Bayview, 31 kilometres north of Sydney, and did not expect to return to the UK as soon as they did in February 1960.[107]

Another on-screen casualty was the Australian actor Ken Goodlet (1921–2006), who played Cobb & Co.'s cranky old head driver Mike Jacky, replaced by Dan Ledward played by Anthony Wickert (Fig. 3.7). 'I never found out exactly what happened there,' Wickert said. 'I guess Ken's character didn't meet American market expectations, so they recast him. They interviewed me and discovered that I could ride a horse. They got me to do a riding test at the police barracks in Paddington and I got the

Fig. 3.7 Ken Goodlet as Mick Jacky (*left*) and Anthony Wickert as Dan Ledward

part based on that.'[108] "Convict Town" (1961) by Dwight Newton was Wickert's first episode, which was also the first episode shown in Melbourne on GTV-9 on 18 February 1961 at 7:00 p.m.[109] "Act of Courage" (1961) by Gerry Day was the first episode shown in Sydney on ATN-7 also on 18 February at 7:00 p.m.[110] The reason for showing different episodes in Melbourne and Sydney was probably due to a shortage of copies of the films, as the series predated effective TV networking in Australia.

The Actors and Actresses

A total of 137 Australian actors (111) and actresses (26) guest-starred in *Whiplash*.[111] They included many of the country's best film, radio, stage, and television performers, such as Neva Carr-Glynn (1908–1995), Janette Craig, Stewart Ginn (1922–1971), Reg Gorman (1932–2021), Ron Graham (1926–2020), Margo Lee (1923–1987), Lionel Long (1939–1998), Lew Luton (1933–2018), Moray Powell (1911–1985), Walter Pym (1905–1980), Ron Shand (1906–1993), and Bettina Welch (1922–1993). The problem was finding enough of them to appear in *Whiplash*. 'Those we got were very good, but there just weren't enough of them,'[112] Peter Graves said. In a newspaper article he wrote less than halfway into making the series, he admitted that 'we have run out of actors, and our casting director is bemoaning the fact that he doesn't have more.'

To date, our casting problem is so acute that in the 14 completed episodes, we have gone through the roster of available Aussie actors, using some of them as many as three and four times. It's a standard joke back in Hollywood, "Don't call us, we'll call you," but believe me, just about 30 Hollywood actors here would stand us in great stead. I want to add that this is no reflection on the calibre of actors in Australia. It is due entirely to the fact that, with so little production going on, there is no great demand for the talents of actors.[113]

The shortage of Australian actors and actresses caused a headache for Ben Fox. He believed that an actor should not appear in the same series in different roles more than three times,[114] but the lack of local talent forced him to break his own rule. Aboriginal elder and actor Robert Tudawali (1929–1967), who played Marbuck in the Australian film *Jedda* (1955), portrayed seven characters in *Whiplash*—more than anyone else. He was Roonga in "Barbed Wire," Dalgowlie in "The Bone That Whispered," a tribesman in "Dutchman's Reef," Kogarah in "Fire Rock" (1961) by Michael Plant, Mundaru in "The Hunters," Kuanspa in "The Magic Wire," and Kuraba in "The Wreckers" (1961) by Daphne Field. Anthony Wickert thought the producers did not give Uncle Robert the respect he deserved. Instead of booking him into a nice hotel when he came to Sydney, they would put him up at the studio.[115] Also, newspapers sometimes deliberately cast Uncle Robert in a bad light. For example, gratuitously tacked onto the end of an already questionable story in *The Sydney Morning Herald* about Aboriginals wanting to break into Fannie Bay gaol, near Darwin, to get 'the best Christmas tucker in the Territory' was the following malicious information: 'A great welcome was given to aboriginal actor Robert Tudawali when he returned from filming the TV series *Whiplash*. Tudawali spent last Christmas in gaol for supplying liquor to another Aboriginal.'[116]

Fox and John Meredyth Lucas finally rose above the rivalry between Sydney and Melbourne and travelled south to recruit some new faces for *Whiplash*'s last seven episodes. The Melbourne actors Peter Aanensen, who played the policeman-turned-publican Jim Bacon in the Australian TV soap opera *Bellbird* (1967–1977), and Terry McDermott (1928–2018), best known for playing Detective Sergeant Frank Bronson in the Australian police TV series *Homicide* (1964–1977), were both signed to appear in the episode "The Magic Wire" by Ralph W. Peterson. The Aboriginals are stopping the delivery of building materials to the company installing the overland telegraph because someone told them it was to blame for the drought. Suspicion falls on the building contractor, Jack Sheridan (McDermott), who will avoid financial penalties if the Aboriginals cause delays to construction. But the troublemaker turns out to be the quartermaster, Sam Green (Aanensen), who will profit from selling replacement supplies. The Aboriginal elder and actor Tjunkata "Nosepeg" Tjupurrula (c.1918–1993) also appeared in this episode. 'He was picked out in Alice Springs earlier this year by an Artransa film unit taking pictures of tribal dances for the *Whiplash* series,' *The Sydney Morning Herald* reported. 'He was flown to Sydney two weeks ago and will soon begin acting the part of an aboriginal tribesman in an episode called "The Magic Wire," which tells the fictitious story of linking Brisbane and Sydney by telegraph.'[117] Uncle Tjunkata arrived at Kingsford Smith Airport dressed in a loincloth and wearing full body paint.[118] Of all of *Whiplash*'s actors, he intrigued Graves the most. 'After spending a day before the camera, Nosepeg wanted to change his name to John Carter. "No fooling," said Peter, "he felt the name Carter gave him more dignity as an actor."'[119] Besides acting, Uncle Tjunkata was also an activist and a painter. However, like many people in those days, *Whiplash*'s cast and crew tended to look down on Aboriginals. For example, Graves told Charles Witbeck: 'They drink out of their hands—wouldn't know what a cup is for.'[120] Of course, this patronising remark was not true.

The best-known Australian actor to guest-star in *Whiplash* was Chips Rafferty (1909–1971), who was renowned for playing "typical Australian" characters. His film credits included many Australian Westerns, such as *The Overlanders* (1946), *Bitter Springs*, *Kangaroo*, and *The Sundowners* (1960), as well as the World War II military drama *The Desert Rats* (1956), and the eighteenth-century naval drama *Mutiny on the Bounty* (1962) directed by Lewis Milestone. Rafferty also appeared in several American TV series, such as *Gunsmoke*, *The Wackiest Ship in the Army* (1965–1966), *The Big Valley* (1965–1969), *The Girl from U.N.C.L.E.* (1966–1967), and *The Monkees* (1966–1968). He appeared in two episodes of *Whiplash*: "The Adelaide Arabs" by Ralph W. Peterson and "Day of the Hunter" by Don Ingalls. In "The Adelaide Arabs," for example, Rafferty played a bushranger named Sorrel, who—along with O'Hara (Chuck Faulkner) and Link (Don Barkham)—rob Chris Cobb on his way to an auction in Adelaide, South Australia, to bid for three Arabian stallions. Virginia Jessup (Coralie Neville, 1924–2009) then purchases the horses since Cobb has no money to bid. But the Sorrel gang steals them from her to

Fig. 3.8 Chips Rafferty as Sorrel (*left*) and Peter Graves as Chris Cobb on the set of "The Adelaide Arabs"

use in a bank robbery, incriminating Cobb by leaving his stolen wallet behind. But instead of arresting him for horse stealing, Lieutenant Hoffman (Stuart Wagstaff, 1925–2015) teams up with him to hunt down the Sorrel gang and return the stallions to Jessup, who is so grateful for Cobb's help that she presents him with one of the Adelaide Arabs. Graves thought Rafferty was 'the best of the Australian actors,'[121] while Wickert 'smiled at the thought of working with him. We played chess in the downtime on the set. Chips wasn't the typical Australian character you saw on the screen,'[122] he said (Fig. 3.8).

Male characters usually dominated *Whiplash*, but in the episode "Sarong" by Gene Roddenberry it is the female characters. The local MP,

Oscar Wenders (John Tate, 1915–1979), informs Chris Cobb that female indentured servants from the islands are disappearing while travelling on one particular Cobb & Co. route. So, with Dan Ledward driving instead of the corrupt driver, Cobb pretends to be a passenger on the stagecoach. The others on board are four "Asian" women (Barbara Guest, Dale Ford, Leilani Kemp, and Willi Koopman, b.1944) under the control of a law broker named Hennessy (Julian Flett, 1923–2005). At an unscheduled coach stop, Ledward pretends to shoot Cobb before Capart (John Fegan, 1908–1981) takes Hennessy and the women to a secret pearl farm run by the evil Lucien Zumwalt (Joe McCormick), since 'women make the best pearl divers,' according to him. Cobb follows them, but Hennessy and Capart capture him. Zumwalt orders them to feed Cobb to the sharks, but they fall overboard and are eaten instead. In the meantime, the women kidnapped by Zumwalt overpower him and hand him over to Cobb. (Some of Sydney's top fashion models played the feisty captives, including Janet Brearly, Winsome Gooi, Marilyn Gregory, Susan Smith, Kaia Stanford, Kay Stubbs, Ann Taylor, and Natalie Thomas.) Later, Cobb tells Wenders the women are now running the pearl farm as a cooperative—striking an early blow for Women's Lib. "Sarong" also showcases *Whiplash*'s weird and wonderful faux geography. As a result of filming different scenes in geographically diverse places such as Alice Springs, French's Forrest, and the Northern Beaches region of Sydney and then putting them together later, in some episodes arid desert, dense bush, and sandy beaches are depicted existing cheek-by-jowl.

Presenting Aboriginal Culture

On 14 May 1960, 22 members of *Whiplash*'s cast and crew flew to Alice Springs (Aboriginal name Mparntwe), Northern Territory, 2000 kilometres northeast of Sydney, to film six episodes of the series over six weeks (not 10 days as was reported[123]), including some all-purpose views of the spectacular Central Australian landscape to insert in other episodes. 'We will film the beauty of the McDonnell Rangers [Tjoritja], Ayers Rock [Uluru] with its aboriginal myths and legends, the beauties of Ormiston Gorge [Kwartatuma], the Ross River, and other scenic spots around Alice Springs,'[124] *Whiplash*'s unit manager Ron Whelan (1905–1965) said. 'Going to Alice Springs to film was like a wonderful holiday,' Anthony Wickert recalled. 'It was a truly educational experience. I'd never been anywhere like that in my life before. It opened my eyes to Australia.'[125]

Fig. 3.9   The Alice Springs Hotel (c.1959)

However, it was not all beer and skittles, especially for the cast and crew who stayed at the unglamorous Alice Springs Hotel (Fig. 3.9). According to John Meredyth Lucas:

> It was [made] of cement—all bare cement, lobby, halls, rooms. We had one of the few rooms with a private bath. In the centre of our large bedroom hung a single light bulb on the end of a cord. The bathroom contained the requisite washbowl, toilet and shower. The odd aspect of the shower is that it had no enclosure. Water came out of the showerhead and spurted all over the bathroom, basin, toilet, everything. The bathroom being a step up from the bedroom, surplus water ran down onto the cement floor beneath the bed where a drain had been provided for that problem. The hotel food was god-awful. Australia had recently relaxed its white only immigration policy and had begun to let in southern Europeans so excellent Greek and Italian restaurants were beginning to spring up.[126]

In 1960, the British toy company Bell made a board game based on *Whiplash* that acknowledged the importance of Alice Springs to the series. The idea is that Chris Cobb despatches two, three, or four stagecoaches (each representing a player) from Alice Springs. They pick up quantities of gold (cardboard tokens) along the way from "Bush Town," "Gun City," and "River Creek." The coaches travel through territory inhabited by bushrangers, who can steal their gold. The game ends when the first coach arrives back at Alice Springs, and the player with the most gold wins the game. A photograph of a Cobb & Co. stagecoach with the McDonnell Ranges in the background decorates the box. The series generated very little merchandise, but this board game was well done.

In my view, the episodes of *Whiplash* that focus on Aboriginal culture and feature Aboriginal actors are the most interesting—and also the most troubling. For example, the episode "The Bone That Whispered" (1961) by Michael Plant, filmed in Central Australia, explores 'becoming aboriginal.'[127] An Aboriginal tracker named Billy Jo (Henry Murdoch, 1920–1987) thinks a renegade tribe of Aboriginals has ambushed Dan Ledward. He tells Chris Cobb that Edwin Regnor (Nigel Lovell, 1916–2001), a white man who was wrongly accused of murder and sentenced to death but escaped and joined this tribe, has taught them to hate all white men. At the same time, Regnor's daughter Marianne (Gwenda Pippen, b.1952) turns up to ask Cobb to find her father. Cobb finds Regnor, tells him his conviction will be overturned, and convinces him to return to Sydney after helping him find Ledward. But the tribe's magic chief is angry with Regnor for sparing Ledward and Cobb's lives and condemns him to death by "pointing the bone." He and Cobb find Ledward, but Regnor's health is failing fast. Only the more powerful magic chief Tjalkalieri (Jack Kelly—not of *Maverick* fame) can save him, but they do not know where to find him. Then Regnor's tribal "brother" Dalgowlie (Robert Tudawali) turns up with Tjalkalieri, who saves his life by mystifyingly removing a bone from his chest. Thus, Regnor survived two death sentences—the first one for murder imposed by white society and the second for showing mercy imposed by black society.

At first glance, especially on black and white television, it appears that white actor Nigel Lovell was wearing blackface. However, he was a white man who wanted to become Aboriginal, covering his body with red ochre (also used by the Aboriginals ritually) to help him assimilate into his adopted tribe, and not blackface makeup. So, when Regnor leaves the tribe and returns to Sydney, he washes off the red ochre. On the other hand, in the episode "The Legacy" (1961) by Bill Templeton, white actor Reg Livermore (b.1938) did wear blackface to play Maloomba, a runaway Aboriginal youth. It was a bad mistake by the producers, as the role should

Fig. 3.10 Reg Livermore as Maloomba (*left*) and Peter Graves as Chris Cobb in "The Legacy"

have been played by an Aboriginal actor, especially as *Whiplash* was the first TV series to employ Aboriginal actors[128] and made a big point of using "the real McCoy." Livermore became Australia's leading burlesque performer, best known for his notorious one-person show, "Betty Blockk Buster Follies" (1975). In 2022 I asked the 83-year-old actor to reflect on his role in *Whiplash* as a 22-year-old actor:

> I have to say *Whiplash* was not my favourite assignment. As for playing the young bloke, Maloomba, my casting would not pass muster now that we know. But way back then, the Tivoli Theatre was presenting revivals of "The Black and White Minstrel Show." And in 1954, I saw a ballet called "Corroboree" at a Royal Command performance in the presence of Her Majesty the Queen by an all-white Australian ballet company. Each dancer was in blackface and got up in some form of tribal paint, stomping about brandishing spears or boomerangs. It is always an uncomfortably embarrassing experience watching actors who are not suitable for their roles, let alone stretching audience credibility when white actors venture into matters of cultural representation. I did feel uneasy as Maloomba, but not because of the colour they painted me, but because I had to ride a horse. I had never been near one before, and I was terrified! However, I have no doubt my appearance was likewise ridiculous. Scared or not, embarrassed or not, I was

just another young actor attempting to make his way, to earn a living. God knows, there was little enough work to go around back then, and performers were happy to take what they could get. It was a job, pure and simple. But I wasn't pushing would-be Aboriginal actors out of the way to secure my role. I wasn't even aware of any Aboriginal actors at the time—apart from those we saw in the Australian film *Jedda*. The stock-in-trade traditional theatrical repertoire and casting dominating the theatre back then didn't call for them.[129]

In her book *Blackface* (2021), the African American author Ayanna Thompson (b.1972) argued that concerning theatre, film, and television, blackface makes playing black "white property."[130] Having been put in a hopeless, no-win situation by the producers of *Whiplash*, Reg Livermore's defence for playing Maloomba is a common one: innocence through ignorance based on acceptable behaviour at the time.[131] While I understand his point of view and do not doubt his sincerity, the fact is that blackface is wrong and must be denounced under all circumstances, no matter when.

The episode "Rider on the Hill" by Harry Julian Fink involves Indigenous magic. An Aboriginal "death stick" is left anonymously on Cobb & Co.'s doorstep for Chris Cobb. Dan Ledward says anybody who gets one is supposed to die before the next full moon. Cobb and Ledward then head off on a long journey with a stagecoach full of passengers: a young woman named Helen Tanner (Delia Williams, b.1930), a murderer named Morgan (Eric Reiman, d.1975) off to the gallows and his police escort (Ivor Bromley, 1918–1970), a swagman named Carthy (Gordon Glenwright, 1918–1985), and an Aboriginal labourer named Chengra (John Cadell, 1920–1993). Naturally, suspicion over the death stick falls on him. In conversation with Helen Tanner, Chris Cobb reveals he killed the Sorley brothers while they were holding up his stagecoach. Why should Morgan hang and Cobb live for committing the same crime, Tanner reasonably wonders? On their first night sleeping under the stars, someone shoots at Cobb but misses. It turns out to be Carthy, the father of the Sorley brothers, who also sent him the death stick. He tries to kill Cobb again the following night when the moon is full, but Chengra spears him in the back just before he can. Dying on the ground, Carthy implores Tanner to kill Cobb because she is his daughter and the Sorley brothers' sister.

"Barbed Wire" is another episode by Fink that also involves Indigenous magic. A wealthy grazier named John Dundee (Grant Taylor, 1917–1971) sends some thugs led by Walt Sullivan (Eric Reiman) to whip a struggling farmer named Joe Pearce (Phillip Ross, b.1929) for erecting barbed wire fences on his land. Two of Dundee's men also stop Chris Cobb and Dan Ledward from delivering bails of barbed wire to other farmers. When they threaten to shoot, Cobb kills one (Don Barkham, 1935–2012), but the other shoots Ledward in the leg. They seek help at Pearce's house, only to find him injured and in need of help too. Dundee then sends Sullivan to tell Cobb to get rid of the barbed wire and leave. Of course, he refuses, so they fight using whips. (It is very similar to Connor and Gamble's fight with whips in *Kangaroo*.) The next day, Pearce's juvenile son Bobby (Brett Hart) takes a gun and rides to Dundee's place, so he and Cobb follow him. Dundee orders them to leave, which they do, only to be ambushed by him and his men on their way back. Dundee orders Roonga (Robert Tudawali), one of his Aboriginal stockmen, to use Indigenous magic to paralyse Cobb, telling Sullivan to shoot him while he is defenceless. When Sullivan refuses, Dundee shoots him and aims at Cobb. Roonga is angry with Dundee for killing Sullivan and not letting Cobb and the Pearces go, so he uses Indigenous magic to paralyse Dundee so they can escape. (John Meredyth Lucas later named his family's pet dog, an Australian Kelpie, "Roonga" after Tudawali's character.[132])

It is difficult to vouch for the authenticity of the Aboriginal culture presented in *Whiplash*, even when Aboriginal actors were involved. It is mainly because the episodes were written by non-Aboriginal "others," especially Hollywood scriptwriters who had never been to Australia and probably did their research in the Los Angeles Public Library. *Whiplash*'s local expert on Aboriginal culture was David Eastman, who had worked for nine years with the Australian Government Film Unit and spent a lot of time in the Outback. I am sure he meant well, but the racist attitudes of the day influenced his advice. One episode of *Whiplash*, for example, called for the Aboriginal actors to perform a dance involving spear-throwing. However, they danced about the arrival of the TV crew instead. Eastman had to sort it out. After consulting widely with experts, he decided 'the only way to film the dance sequences was by re-teaching the "missionised" natives,' as they had 'forgotten much of their native culture.'[133] We now know this is incorrect. Nor was integrating current events and popular culture into Indigenous dance new. For example, in 1937, the Australian explorer Michael Terry (1899–1981) reported that after seeing a Mickey Mouse cartoon at the cinema, an Aboriginal camel-handler named Lockey had 'made himself quite famous at Horseshoe Bend, inventing a new corroboree. […] Made up all black and white, he hops about just like that darned mouse and squeaks for all the world like Mickey,'[134] Terry said.

Danger!

There seems to have been a worrying lack of safety on the *Whiplash* set. While making "Dark Runs the Sea" by Oscar Millard, for example, Joe McCormick was nearly killed in a firearms accident. Arnold Lofton (McCormick), a crooked magistrate, teams up with Raike Dartner (Guy Doleman, 1923-1996), a ruthless murderer, to kidnap Lofton's niece Fiona Merrick (Annette Andre). Chris Cobb and Dan Ledward go searching for her because she disappeared while waiting for a Cobb & Co. coach. But Dartner captures them and keeps them prisoners in a makeshift animal shelter, belonging to an eccentric naturalist named Bradley Bradley (Reg Lye, 1912-1987). In the meantime, Merrick has fallen in love with Dartner, who promises to use his share of the ransom money to sail away with her. However, when he turns out to be a brute, she and Bradley help Cobb and Ledward to escape. In the ensuing cuffuffle, Ledward shoots Lofton point-blank in the stomach, while Dartner drowns in the river trying to flee Cobb.

'I was delighted with [McCormick's] performance,' John Meredyth Lucas said. 'He jerked back with the impact and then fell in a crumpled heap. It was perfect. "Cut," I yelled. "That was beautiful."'[135] But when McCormick rolled over, clutching his stomach, he was horrified to see blood on his fingers. The prop man (Frants Folmer?) had used four times the amount of gunpowder required, which turned the wad of cardboard that held the gunpowder in place in the shell into a "bullet." McCormick was hospitalised for a fortnight with a hole an inch deep in his stomach.[136] 'Obviously, whoever was in charge of props didn't check it out correctly,' Andre said. 'That was inexperience.'[137]

There were more lapses, though. For example, while filming "Dutchman's Reef" by Gene Roddenberry, Graves and Wickert almost were speared. In this episode, Mrs. Culbert (Queenie Ashton, 1903-1999), a wealthy socialite from Sydney, asks Cobb and Ledward to find her son, Norton "Teddy Bear" Culbert (Leonard Teale, 1922-1994), who ran off and joined a tribe of Aboriginals in the Simpson Desert. Cobb agrees, even though he suspects she wants to find Dutchman's Reef, a rich gold deposit rumoured to be where Norton is "hiding." Members of Norton's tribe steal Cobb and Ledward's horses and guns and empty their canteens, forcing them to hike to the tribe's waterhole. But in exchange for getting some water, the head of the tribe decrees that Norton will get three chances to kill Cobb. After his first two spears only narrowly miss him,

Cobb feels compelled to remind Norton he once saved his life in a barroom brawl. Norton then puts down his last spear, telling Cobb he does not wish to return to his mother because he is happy living as a tribesman in the bush. Before they leave Norton in peace, Cobb stumbles on a large gold nugget, indicating that it is Dutchman's Reef. In Sydney, Cobb "protects" Norton by telling his mother he is dead and saying nothing about the gold.

Teale thought he had perfected his spear-throwing for the attack on Graves and Wickert at the water hole, deliberately missing by a large margin for safety reasons during rehearsals. However, his accuracy had improved alarmingly by the time they filmed the scene, only narrowly missing them, while Wickert cut his head avoiding a spear.[138] The episode was shot at Wigley Waterhole on a cattle station run by Robert Darken (1919–2000). 'We flew from Sydney to Adelaide to Alice Springs. It was fascinating. Oh, I loved it,'[139] said Joan Endress, who accompanied Graves there. But their absence was sorely felt by their daughters back at Avalon Beach. 'They left us behind with the babysitter for six weeks, which was really tough,' Kelly Graves told me. 'You're already far away from home, and now your folks have gone away too.'[140]

Finally, Annette Andre almost drowned during the filming of "Storm River" by Don Ingalls. In this episode, Cobb is knocked out and robbed by a masked man while tending to his horse during a violent storm. He wakes up in an out-of-the-way cottage belonging to the novelist John Kerrabee (Grant Taylor), who lives with his beast of a son Cloy (Norman Erskine, 1931–2010), and a 17-year-old girl named Cassie (Andre). It turns out that Cloy hit Cobb and stole his money belt, which causes a ferocious argument between father and son. Cassie wants to escape the Kerrabees' macho household and study dressmaking in Sydney, but Cobb refuses to take her with him when he leaves the next day. With the roads flooded by the storm, Cobb must navigate a snake-infested river in an outrigger canoe. As Cassie has developed a crush on Cobb, she sails after him. Then Cloy sails after her, and John sails after him. While fleeing a poisonous water snake, Cassie falls overboard and is rescued by Cobb before the Kerrabees finally catch them. Jealous of Cassie's affection for Cobb, Cloy takes a potshot at him, then they fight each other using pole hooks—yet another unconventional weapon. Finally, John allows Cassie to travel to Sydney with Cobb to study dressmaking. Since Andre could not swim, John Meredyth Lucas had told her that a stunt double would do the scene.

When we went to shoot it and I asked where the double was, they said 'we haven't got one.' I said, 'I can't swim—I really mean it.' But I was told it was shallow and I'd be able to stand up. So, when the moment came, I took a deep breath and threw myself into the water. I went down and down and down and then I did come up but went down again! When I came up the second time, Peter [Graves] was ashen and grabbed me by the dress and yanked me up into the canoe—it wasn't very elegant—but they kept that shot in.'[141]

Valerie Taylor (née Heighes, b.1935) was supposed to be Andre's stunt double on that occasion. Before marrying Ron Taylor (m.1963–2012) and becoming a renowned underwater photographer, she was an animator at Press Features Services and sometimes visited the studio where they filmed *Whiplash*. 'Are you here for today's *Whiplash* shoot?' Graves asked Taylor by mistake one day. Her curiosity piqued, one thing led to another and she ended up as a part-time stuntwoman on the series. 'My stunt work started with horse-riding,'[142] Taylor said. 'The director asked if I had any experience with horses. I told him I did, which was not a complete lie—I had been led on a tame pony once. I held on as they filmed and shot the scenes that were needed. I found the galloping horse easy to ride—it was when she slowed down that I became uncomfortable.' Interestingly, Taylor's recollection of what happened on the set of "Storm River" was quite different from Andre's:

> The director again came to me, this time asking if I could paddle a canoe. As I had a canoe at home I could honestly say yes. Approaching a waterfall in my canoe, I wondered if I had perhaps bitten off more than I could chew, but I just held on and persevered and everything worked out beautifully. It was more rapids than a waterfall. The canoe did all the work—I just hung on waving the paddle like an expert.[143]

Stunt doubles were essential to the production of *Whiplash*. On 5 February 1961 two of the series' stunt doubles, Peter Armstrong (1936–2001) and David Bryant, were guests on Sydney TV talk show *Penthouse* (1960–1961) to promote *Whiplash*'s forthcoming debut in Sydney.[144] (Graves had returned to Los Angeles by then.)

THE HORSES AND STAGECOACHES

Lionel Ware owned a livery stable in Leichardt, five kilometres west of Sydney, and specialised in supplying and training horses for the entertainment industry. In 1959 he was working on two Australian Westerns at the same time: the TV series *Whiplash* and the film *The Sundowners*, starring Hollywood "royalty" Deborah Kerr (1921–2007) and Robert Mitchum (1917–1997), which was being made in South Australia. Initially, Ware wanted his 14-year-old son Grahame Ware, who had just left school, to tend the horses for *The Sundowners*. 'South Australia! That'll be great!' Grahame excitedly told his parents.

> Then Mum said to Dad, 'He might not come home if he goes over there—he wants to see a bit of the country.' So, a week before I was to leave, Dad came up to me and said, 'I'm going to put you on *Whiplash* because it's for 12 months, and *The Sundowners* is only for three months.' I lived on my own, for 12 months, in the town they built in the scrub—you wouldn't have even known it was there! My father would let me have one mate stay over at the weekend, but one weekend I decided to have all of my mates over, and I got into a lot of trouble—Dad gave me a real hiding![145]

Looking after the horses for *Whiplash* kept Grahame busy. Several months before filming started, he began training the horses to ignore gunfire and get used to a boom microphone by galloping them with a tin dangling from the end of a stick in front of their noses.[146] 'If you school your horses and work them properly, you can do anything with them, and they listen to you,' Grahame said. 'Any horses with no brains, you get rid of them.'[147]

Grahame began work at 6:00 a.m., grooming the horses for the day of filming ahead, maintaining the harnesses and saddles, and taking the horses for a swim in a nearby waterhole on hot days. Sometimes, he also coached the actors and actresses on how to ride. 'They have to be able to pass a riding test given by Dad,' Grahame said. 'If they couldn't ride, we would give them a small horse that was easy—all they had to do was steer. But if they could ride quite well, we'd give them a smarter horse.'[148] While Peter Graves had lessons when he first arrived to get used to the big piebald horse he rode in *Whiplash*, he did most of the riding himself in the series. At least he knew his limitations, declaring unashamedly: 'A guy is no good to a film outfit with a broken leg, so a stuntman fills in some of the risky stuff.'[149]

Grahame also appeared as an extra in some episodes of *Whiplash*. 'I've played a few bit parts and have been the stand-in for various people,' he told Diane Roberts of *The Australian Women's Weekly*. 'I've also been in a lot of episodes driving horses and buggies through the town, and once I was an aboriginal,' he said. 'I was painted black, sitting in a canoe on the Manly Dam.'[150] As mentioned, this would be unacceptable today. Grahame earned 13 pounds 10 shillings (£13/10/-) per week in wages,[151] which does not sound like very much today, but it was well above what most 14-year-old boys earned in 1959–1960.

Lionel Ware also supplied the Cobb & Co. stagecoaches for *Whiplash*. 'My father got an original Cobb & Co. coach from the Bathurst area and brought it home, but it was so far gone, he sold it to the Cobb & Co. restaurant in Tempe [nine kilometres south of Sydney]. So, with the help of the museum in Sydney, we got two coaches made the same,' Grahame said. 'We put plenty of work into the five-horse team that pulled the coach. They were a brilliant team, automatic. One day, when Peter Maxwell was directing, they had a big tree across the road, and the three leading horses jumped the tree, and the two pole-horses behind them skidded into it. There could've been a bad accident. The pole horses could've broken their legs if they had hit it real hard, but the leaders just jumped over it, like a hurdle, and stopped. When you do movies with horses, you do have accidents. It was two o'clock in the afternoon, and Peter Maxwell said, "That's it. We're going home. It's the best shot of this show. I'm as happy as Larry—we've done it in one take!"'[152]

Driving a Cobb & Co. coach was no mean feat. 'I had some rough times on those stagecoaches,' Graves said. 'I could have died a thousand times.'[153] But he and Anthony Wickert were always under Lionel's watchful eye. 'Do you know where he was during the stagecoach sequences?' Wickert asked me. 'He was under the front seat of the coach! He had a huge asset in the horses and the coaches, so he was very wary to mind it. They could have easily tipped over.'[154] Later, they used stagecoaches to promote the series. 'Shoppers stared as a vehicle out of the past, a Cobb & Co. coach drawn by five horses and carrying a "shotgun guard," rattled down George Street, [Sydney,] yesterday,'[155] *The Sydney Morning Herald* reported. It was publicising *Whiplash*, premiering on ATN Channel 7 at 7:00 p.m. the following day (Saturday 18 February 1961). When Lionel died aged 48 in 1965, Grahame took over the livery stable. He still has *Whiplash*'s two Cobb & Co. stagecoaches (Fig. 3.11).

Fig. 3.11 Anthony Wickert as Dan Ledward (*left*) and Peter Graves as Chris Cobb driving a stagecoach

THE STUDIO AND THE SET

Making *Whiplash* seemed like a safe bet. Not only were Westerns the most popular type of show on television during the 1950s and 1960s, but they were also the most numerous. When the American TV Western *Tales of Wells Fargo* premiered with some fanfare in Australia on 5 May 1958, ten other American Western TV series were also being shown in Sydney: (1) *The Wild West Show*; (2) *The Roy Rogers Show* (1951–1957); (3) *Hopalong Cassidy* (1952–1954); (4) *Tombstone Territory*; (5) *The Life and Legend of Wyatt Earp* (1955–1961); (6) *Cheyenne* (1955–1963); (7) *Gunsmoke*; (8) *Sugarfoot* (1957–1961); (9) *Have Gun Will Travel*; and (10) *Wagon Train* (1957–1965).[156] But it really was a risk because Australia's television industry was still in its infancy and not equipped to produce such an ambitious series as *Whiplash*.

Even though Artransa was the best film studio in Australia, it was well below Hollywood standards, which the Americans certainly noticed. Peter Graves said it was naïve of them to have assumed they would find 'another Hollywood down there as far as facilities and production know-how were concerned.'[157] John Meredyth Lucas was blunter. 'Artransa was not what we would call a studio,'[158] he said. One particular incident settled it for him: on 10 October 1960, the dense bush surrounding Artransa caught fire. However, Lucas could not find one cameraman at the studio to film the spectacular blaze:

> 'We could see gigantic flames licking up the tall trees,' he said. 'When they reached the tops the fire would crown—explode like the Fourth of July, spewing fire in all directions and catching the adjacent trees. I wanted a camera. God, with a spectacle like that, I would write an episode to use it in. Our cameraman had not started work and could not be reached by phone. I kept bugging the busy firefighters. Wasn't there anyone who could use the cameras in the department? There wasn't. I am fine with a still camera, but I knew I could never manage a large motion picture camera. While the battle to save the studio went on, I went through lists in the studio manager's office, calling cameramen. I got one who promised he would come "straightaway." I was delighted until I learned he lived in Hornsby, at the very end of the North Shore railway. My mind was already developing a story of our stagecoach caught in a catastrophic fire. When the cameraman finally arrived, the studio was safe and the fire had already burned itself out. We could see flames in the distance and smouldering stumps in the foreground. I never got my fire episode.'[159]

The Americans also had trouble with the local carpenters who constructed *Whiplash*'s sets. Being used to building houses and not theatrical sets meant to be quickly knocked down to make room for the next one, they 'insisted on immortalising each set with hundreds of 10-inch spikes to hold it together!' Don Ingalls said. 'You couldn't dynamite one of their sets down! If we remonstrated or tried to explain, they calmly told us what to do with the set, mate, and huffed back to the house-building trade from whence they came.'[160]

The same carpenters built a replica of a nineteenth-century Australian gold rush town on 139 acres leased from the Savoy Corporation Ltd., a Melbourne-based property developer, at Oxford Falls about a mile from Artransa.[161] It was named Fury Creek (perhaps an inside joke referring to Graves' previous TV series, *Fury*), although it served as every small town

Fig. 3.12   Workmen constructing Fury Creek (1959)

in *Whiplash*. Peter Mullins designed the TV town based on historic photographs of Bathurst dating from Cobb & Co.'s days (Fig. 3.12).[162] It had about 20 buildings, including a Bank of New South Wales, a blacksmith's, a billiard saloon, a chaff-and-grain store, Cobb & Co.'s office, a doctor's, a draper's, a hotel, a police station, and stables. There were also bark huts, corrugated-iron humpies, farmhouses, gold diggings, mullock heaps, and tents outside of the town.

Fury Creek was built from scratch using recycled bricks, corrugated iron, timber, wrought iron, and so on. 'Artransa has for months been the biggest buyer of second-hand building materials in Sydney, for the "town" has to appear suitably weathered in the series,'[163] Bill Olson said. Mullins was also willing to move old buildings to the site—if only he could have bought some. For example, he had his eye on an old slab hut on a farm near Sydney, but when he spoke to the owner, their conversation went as follows:

Mullins: I'm interested in that old slab hut you've got in your paddock. Are you using it?
Owner: Aw, no. She's been empty for a while now.

Mullins: Well, I'm from a film company and we're looking for a hut like that to use in a picture. I'd like to buy it from you.
Owner: No mate, don't think I'll sell her.
Mullins: But why? We'll pay a good price. Anyway, the thing is nearly falling over.
Owner: Well mate, I'll tell you; I've been meaning to straighten her up for a while now. Might do it soon.
Mullins: But what's the use of straightening it if you're not going to use it?
Owner: Aw well, you never know. She might come into some use one of these days. Don't you worry, I'll straighten her up all right and then we'll see.
Mullins: Well, you won't sell. Is that the position?
Owner: No mate, might as well leave her where she is.[164]

In the end, Mullins built a new slab hut from 'slabs cut in the Wyong hills and freighted to Sydney.'[165] He also fitted out the buildings with appropriate furniture, firearms, old photographs, and kerosene lamps, among others. It did not come cheap: Fury Creek cost £30,000 to build.[166] Naturally, it caused a lot of public interest: 'The doings at French's Forest, where a town was built, and the film company had its headquarters, soon became local news, and televiewers have been anxious to see it,'[167] Nan Musgrove said. So, when production ended in 1960, many people naturally wondered what would happen to Fury Creek. '"Well," began Ben Fox—this was something he was keen to announce—"I believe it is to be preserved and made into a sort of Frontierland, like the one at Disneyland in America,"' he told Kenneth Brass of *The Sydney Morning Herald*. '"There are to be horse rides, stagecoach rides, and a restaurant is to be erected. 'Bushrangers' will be there to hold up the stages."'[168]

Unfortunately, it did not happen—the site was used for houses[169]—and Sydney missed out on its "Frontierland." However, Fury Creek demonstrated you could *recreate* Australian history and not just *preserve* it. Indeed, I suspect that it played a significant—albeit unacknowledged— role as a model for many folk museums that sprung up around Australia after *Whiplash*, like the Pioneer Settlement (1966–present) in Swan Hill, Victoria, one of the first.[170] Designed by the Australian architect Roy Grounds (1905–1981) and the British-Australian art director Dr. Eric Westbrook (1915–2005), who were working together on the new building (1968) for the National Gallery of Victoria in Melbourne, the Pioneer Settlement is basically a larger version of Fury Creek. It consists of 50

Fig. 3.13 Shops at the Pioneer Settlement, Swan Hill, Victoria (1970s)

buildings, including a bank, a bakery, a chemist's, a post office (that doubles as Cobb & Co.'s office), a hairdresser's, and a saddlery.

Lew Grade's company ATV owned Artransa, which it had purchased specifically for making TV series in Australia for the international market like *Whiplash*. But all of the problems which had dogged that series unnerved ATV, prompting it to sell the studio in July 1960 to the Sydney TV station ATN-7.[171] 'My company still retains an association with [...] Artransa [...] through its shareholding in ATN,' said the chairman of ATV in Australia, Mr. J.D. Patience, trying to sound as positive as he could. 'Reflecting the usual pattern in America and England for telefilm production companies to hire studio facilities when required, ATV's production of *Whiplash* will continue at the Artransa Studios. It means there will be no interruption in the production of *Whiplash*, financed by ATV and destined for worldwide release.'[172] No doubt the producers of the series were relieved to hear that. However, selling Artransa from under them, as it were, must have damaged the cast and crew's morale, as they were indirectly responsible, but not really to blame.

The Critics

Having endured many trials and tribulations to make *Whiplash*, nobody was happier to see the first episode on television than producer Ben Fox. 'Have you ever been to a cocktail party where everyone was, frankly and unashamedly, glued to the television set?' asked "Di," the gossip columnist at *The Sydney Morning Herald*. 'That's what happened at Ben Fox's home [...] at Palm Beach last night when the first episode was shown on TV. While champagne corks popped, Ben told the guests, most of whom played leading roles in the series, that [the Australian actor] Ray Barrett, who's been watching the show for the past four months in London [... said] it was a great success ... and that "I enjoyed seeing all my old friends in it."'[173] *Whiplash* premiered in the UK on 10 September 1960, while the series was still in production in Australia. It got off to a great start over there, being the second-highest rated show on television behind the American private-eye TV series *77 Sunset Strip* (1958–1964).[174] Its initial overseas success prompted some TV critics to suggest that 'in *Whiplash*, the dreams of producers to be able to finance and carry out productions in unfamiliar climes, insofar as North American audiences are concerned, and still come up with first-class entertainment, may well have been realised.'[175] Fox even hinted at making a second series of *Whiplash* to be filmed partly in Hollywood. 'As Cobb was an American, we may find it worthwhile to make a number of films in an American setting before returning to Australia,'[176] he said. This might have been interesting, but it never happened.

Whiplash was damned with faint praise by most TV critics. For example, the Australian TV critic Valda Marshall described it as 'a good old-fashioned Western romp. It was no worse than most of its American counterparts and a good deal better than some.'[177] Similarly, the Canadian TV critic Bob Shiels said: 'In many respects, *Whiplash* [...] is just another cowboy show. [...] The show is crude in many ways, but in other ways, it's different. To the extent that it's crude, it's no better than any low-budget Western. To the extent that it's different, it's rather diverting.'[178]

'*Whiplash* was a disappointment to me because I thought it really would go,'[179] said Peter Graves, looking back. In his view, the series 'could have been much, much better. It was kept in the mould of the American show because there was no time for proper research and production planning. The writers here [in America] should have gone down there [to Australia] and really studied the Cobb & Co. era. Not enough was made of Australia itself; we were too often confined to the back-lot.'[180] Even so, *Whiplash* proved to be "a sleeper" in Australia. In 1970, Graves told Donald

Freeman of *The Fort Worth Star Telegram*: 'I did a series in Australia called *Whiplash*, and it was a bomb there the first time around. [...] Now it's going into its third rerun, and the Aussies love it. I have no idea why. Great people, the Australians. If they like you, you're their "mate"—their friend—right off, and they tell you their whole story, and they're buying you a beer which, fortunately, they drink cold.'[181]

Whiplash is a significant but largely forgotten Australian TV series. In my opinion, the standard of acting and production was very high, especially given that the Australian television industry had been going for only three years when they made the series. Perhaps Chris Cobb could have been more of a flawed character, like Paladin (Richard Boone, 1917–1981) in *Have Gun Will Travel*, and Dan Ledward could have been more of a contrast to his boss, like Chester (Dennis Weaver, 1924–2006) in *Gunsmoke*, but they were who they were. That *Whiplash* presented American stories set in Australia is wrong in my view. The inclusion of Australian fauna—albeit too much; Australian landscapes—albeit oddly juxtaposed; and Indigenous culture—albeit well-intended but generally misguided; make them Australian enough for me. My impression is that *Whiplash*'s cast and crew, especially the Americans, felt that life was imitating art and they were living the TV series they were making, as it were. Maybe it was the geographical isolation of Australia in general and Alice Springs in particular. Or perhaps it was the unfamiliar and seemingly inhospitable natural environment—even if we are only talking about blowflies, mosquitoes, spiders, and wet weather. Or possibly the fact that the standard of living in Australia was lower than it was in America back then. Or maybe it was the real dangers faced by the cast while making the series, such as drowning, being shot, or even speared. But whatever it was, post-World War II Australia was the closest thing to the "Wild West" many of the Americans who came here to make *Whiplash* had experienced in real life. As a result, I think they thought the series was more "authentic" than perhaps it was. In any case, while they made mistakes, I believe that *Whiplash* deserves another look and a lot more credit for being the first Australian-made Western TV series.

THE AUTHOR

Derham Groves (b.1956) studied architecture at Deakin University and the Royal Melbourne Institute of Technology (RMIT) and art history at the University of Minnesota. He taught architecture at RMIT from 1985 until 1997 and at the University of Melbourne from 1999 until 2019. Dr. Groves is currently a Senior Fellow in the Faculty of Architecture, Building, and Planning at the University of Melbourne. He is the author of many articles and books about popular culture, architecture, and design, including *Feng-Shui and Western Building Ceremonies* (1991), *You Bastard Moriarty* (1996), *Mail Art: The D-I-Y Letterbox from Workshop to Gatepost* (1998), *TV Houses: Television's Influence on the Australian Home* (2004), *There's No Place Like Holmes: Exploring Sense of Place Through Crime Fiction* (2008), *Victims and Villains: Barbie and Ken Meet Sherlock Holmes* (2009), *Anna May Wong's Lucky Shoes: 1939 Australia Through the Eyes of an Art Deco Diva* (2011), *Out of the Ordinary: Popular Art, Architecture and Design* (2012), *Hopalong Cassidy: A Horse Opera* (2017), *Monkeemania in Australia: Celebrating the 50th Anniversary of The Monkees' Australian Tour in 1968* (2019), *Arthur Purnell's 'Forgotten' Architecture: Canton and Cars* (2020), *Sherlock in the Seventies: A Wild Decade of Sherlock Holmes Films* (2021), and there's more to come!

NOTES

1. 'TV Star Plans New Sequence of Shows,' *The Pensacola News Journal* (Florida), 18 September 1959, p. 14.
2. '2 First-Run Shows Begin,' *Arizona Daily Sun* (Arizona), 15 December 1961, p. 13.
3. K.A. Austin (2006), 'Cobb, Freeman (1830–1878),' *Australian Dictionary of Biography*, https://adb.anu.edu.au/biography/cobb-freeman-3237, accessed 25 September 2021.
4. 'Cobb & Co. Heritage Trail,' https://www.cobbandco.net.au/ accessed 7 October 2021.
5. 'British TV 1950s Filmed Drama: *Whiplash* Starring Peter Graves,' *Dinosaur TV-Save Our Forgotten British Heritage!* http://www.78rpm.co.uk/tvw.htm#d3 accessed 17 February 2021.
6. Bill Olson, 'Chris Cobb Rides Again … There's a Lynch Mob in French's Forest!' *The Sydney Morning Herald* (New South Wales), 8 November 1959, p. 95.
7. 'Crime No.1 TV Theme, "Poor" Commercials,' *The Age* (Victoria), 12 November 1959, p. 26.
8. Nan Musgrove, '2 New Shows: Our Bush Takes a Bow,' *The Australian Women's Weekly* (Australia), 1 March 1961, p. 61.
9. Bill Olson.
10. 'Taming the TV Heroes,' *The Sydney Morning Herald*, 24 January 1960, p. 23.

11. Chuck Faulkner, 'Chuck Faulkner's TOC Column,' *The Sydney Morning Herald*, 29 November 1959, p. 114.
12. Joan Endress, Telephone interview with Derham Groves, 2020.
13. 'Taming the TV Heroes.'
14. Bill Olson.
15. 'Talent Scouts Here for "All Sorts" of Actors,' *The Age*, 21 October 1960, p. 5.
16. Nan Musgrave, 1 March 1961.
17. Stephen Atkinson, 'A Rumble in the Great Australian Silence: *Whiplash* and the Telling of the Australian Frontier,' *ACH: The Journal of the History of Culture in Australia*, 1 January 2007, p. 37.
18. Charles Witbeck, 'A New Western—From Australia!' *The Chicago Tribune* (Illinois), 23 April 1961, p. 423.
19. Charles Gilbert, 'TV Topics: *Whiplash*: Australia's Own Western Series is Now Under Full Production!' *Pix* (Australia), 11 June 1960, pp. 38–43.
20. '*Whiplash* First Australian "Western,"' *Edmonton Journal* (Canada), 14 October 1961, p. 25.
21. 'Made-in-Australia TV "Western" Takes Shape,' *The Age*, 26 November 1959, p. 25.
22. Charles Witbeck, 'Western Has Aussie Flavour: New TV Series Filmed in Australia,' *The Daily Oklahoman* (Oklahoma), 21 May 1961, p. 30.
23. 'Saturday Premiere for *Whiplash*,' *The Sydney Morning Herald*, 13 February 1961, p. 11.
24. "Granny" (aka Sydney Deamer), 'Column 8,' *The Sydney Morning Herald*, 30 January 1961, p. 1.
25. John Meredyth Lucas, *Eighty Odd Years in Hollywood: Memoir of a Career in Film and Television*, Jefferson, North Carolina: McFarland and Company, Inc., Publishers, 2004, p. 216.
26. 'TV Series To Be Filmed at Alice Springs,' *The Beverley Times* (Western Australia), 20 May 1960, p. 5.
27. Anthony Wickert, Telephone interview with Derham Groves, 2020.
28. Stephen Vagg, 'Annette Andre: My Brilliant Early Australian Career,' *Filmlink*, https://www.filmink.com.au/annette-andre/, 29 August 2020, accessed 18 October 2021.
29. Robin Boyd, *The Australian Ugliness*, Melbourne: F.W. Cheshire Pty Ltd., 1960, p. 65.
30. Di Morrissey, *The Silent Country*, Sydney: Pan Macmillan Australia, 2009, p. 14.
31. Ibid.
32. NAA: SP1121/1, Aurness, Peter D.
33. Hedda Hopper, 'Dick Shawn to Make Debut in *Wake Me*,' *The Los Angeles Times* (California) 17 September 1959, p. 54.

34. Joe Finnigan, 'Actor Returns From Abroad, Will Remain,' *The Anderson Herald* (Indiana), 30 October 1960, p. 30.
35. 'T.V. Series to be Filmed at Alice Springs.'
36. Nan Musgrove, '*Open House* Big Success Overseas,' *The Australian Women's Weekly*, 21 October 1959, p. 60.
37. Ibid.
38. '*Whiplash* Moves to New Time, Follows "Dillon" on Tuesdays,' *The Tampa Bay Times* (Florida), 29 December 1961, p. 20.
39. Nan Musgrove, 'American TV Star Here for Australian Western,' *The Australian Women's Weekly*, 14 October 1959, p. 68.
40. Sheilah Graham, 'Arness Near Million—Horton Makes More On Side Than TV,' *The Birmingham News* (Alabama), 17 October 1959, p. 5.
41. Nan Musgrove, 14 October 1959.
42. Mimi Mead, 'Biggest Mission: All is Possible to Peter Graves,' *The Star-Gazette* (New York), 22 June 1968, p. 29.
43. United States Census Bureau, 'Income of Families and Persons in the United States: 1959,' https://www.census.gov/library/publications/1961/demo/p60-035.html, accessed 13 November 2021.
44. Joan Endress.
45. Ibid.
46. Nan Musgrove, 14 October 1959.
47. Joan Endress.
48. Ibid.
49. 'Film Star Is Back,' *The Sydney Morning Herald*, 24 March 1960, p. 31.
50. John Meredyth Lucas, pp. 212–213.
51. Ibid.
52. Joan Endress.
53. Kelly Graves, Telephone interview with Derham Groves, 2020.
54. Geoff Searl, Email to Derham Groves, 12 February 2022.
55. Joan Endress.
56. 'US Actor "Pioneer" in Aust.,' *The Sydney Morning Herald*, 24 October 1960, p. 3.
57. Charles Witbeck, 'Jim Arness's Brother, Peter Graves, Starring in Australian Western,' *The Record* (New Jersey), 22 April 1961, p. 48.
58. Stanley Eichelbaum, 'Peter Graves' Dilemma,' *The San Francisco Examiner* (California), 28 October 1961, p. 10.
59. Ibid.
60. Joseph Finnigan, 'Peter Graves to Star in New Video Series,' *The Herald* (Indiana), 19 November 1962, p. 27.
61. Curiously, Michael Noonan does not mention either *Whiplash* or his co-creator Michael Plant in his autobiography, *In With the Tide: Memoirs of a Storyteller*, St. Lucia: University of Queensland Press, 1995.

62. 'Guide to the Papers of Michael Noonan,' National Library of Australia, https://nla.gov.au/nla.obj-324945336/findingaid accessed 13 October 2021.
63. *The Sydney Morning Herald*, 11 September 1960, p. 116.
64. 'A Film Star's House,' *The Sydney Morning Herald*, 10 July 1960, p. 126.
65. 'New Western Series Has Australian Scene,' *The Hartford Courant* (Connecticut), 12 March 1961, p. 121.
66. Charles Witbeck, 22 April 1961.
67. Bill Olson.
68. Charles Witbeck, 22 April 1961.
69. 'TV Star Plans New Sequence of Shows.'
70. 'Made-In-Australia TV "Western" Takes Shape.'
71. Stephen Vagg, 'Forgotten Australian TV Series: *Whiplash*,' *Filmlink*, https://www.filmink.com.au/forgotten-australian-tv-series-whiplash/, 11 December 2021, accessed 9 February 2022.
72. Robert Vaux, '*Star Trek*: How Gene Roddenberry Drew From a Nearly Forgotten Western,' CBR.com https://www.cbr.com/star-trek-gene-roddenberry-drew-wagon-train/, 13 May 2021, accessed 8 March 2022.
73. Ibid.
74. Joan Endress.
75. Nan Musgrove, 1 March 1961.
76. Di Morrissey, p. 17.
77. Marc Saul (2010), *Whiplash, Television Heaven*, https://television-heaven.co.uk/reviews/whiplash, 12 February 2019, accessed 10 September 2020.
78. Tony Stephens, 'A Midwife at the Birth of TV,' *The Sydney Morning Herald*, https://www.smh.com.au/national/a-midwife-at-the-birth-of-tv-20080130-gdryus.html, 30 January 2008, accessed 17 February 2021.
79. Anthony Wickert.
80. Hedda Hopper, 'Looking at Hollywood: Arness Brothers Going Big in TV, Too,' *The Chicago Tribune*, 23 March 1965, p. 32.
81. 'Coach Drama on TV,' *The Sydney Morning Herald*, 9 August 1959, p. 27.
82. NAA: SP1121/1, Geraghty, Maurice Jean.
83. Nina Gow, Email to Geoff Searl, 12 February 2022.
84. 'Start on Aust. TV "Western,"' *The Age*, 8 October 1959, p. 25.
85. Bill Olson.
86. 'TV Series to be Filmed at Alice Springs.'
87. 'On Location,' *The Age*, 26 November 1959, p. 29.
88. Bill Olson.
89. Terrence O'Flaherty, '"Keep Your Nose Clean" Advice Seems To Have Worked Well,' *The Journal Herald* (Ohio), 18 December 1961, p. 27.
90. Joan Endress.

91. Stephen Vagg, 11 December 2021.
92. David Moore, '*Dinosaur TV*: *Whiplash* Starring Peter Graves,' http://www.78rpm.co.uk/tvw.htm#d3, accessed 25 August 2021.
93. Ibid.
94. *Hartford Courant* (Connecticut), 10 January 1960, p. 114.
95. Sheilah Graham, 'Marlene Will Perform at Dallas State Fair,' *The Evening Star* (Maryland), 19 May 1960, p. 61.
96. Hank Grant, 'For Peter Graves: New Series Planned,' *The Herald and Review* (Illinois), 5 December 1962, p. 19.
97. 'TV Series to be Filmed at Alice Springs.'
98. Hank Grant.
99. Sheilah Graham, 'Hollywood Today: Have a Bash,' *The News Tribune* (Washington), 2 June 1960, p. 16.
100. John Meredyth Lucas, p. 205.
101. Anthony Wickert.
102. Stephen Vagg, 29 August 2020.
103. Stephen Vagg, 11 December 2021.
104. Ibid.
105. David Moore.
106. 'Made-In-Australia TV "Western" Takes Shape.'
107. David Moore.
108. Anthony Wickert.
109. 'Cobb Rides in Feb.,' *The Age*, 26 January 1961, p. 29.
110. '*Whiplash* on ATN,' *The Sydney Morning Herald*, 18 February 1961, p. 5.
111. '*Whiplash* TV Series 1960–1961,' *IMDb*, https://www.imdb.com/title/tt0054577/, accessed 10 September 2020.
112. "US Actor 'Pioneer' in Aust.," *The Sydney Morning Herald*, 24 October 1960, p. 3.
113. Peter Graves, "TV Series Hits Snag," *The Kingsport News* (Tennessee), 29 July 1960, p. 4.
114. "Talent Scouts Here for 'All Sorts' of Actors."
115. Anthony Wickert.
116. 'Christmas In Brief,' *The Sydney Morning Herald*, 24 December 1960, p. 5.
117. 'Meeting a "Long Fella": Nosepeg Got Shock,' *The Sydney Morning Herald*, 27 November 1960, p. 25.
118. 'Contrast in Styles,' *The Sydney Morning Herald*, *The Sydney Morning Herald*, 12 November 1960, p. 6.
119. Charles Witbeck, 22 April 1961, p. 48.
120. Ibid.
121. Joe Finnigan, 'Actor Returns From Abroad, Will Remain,' *The Anderson Herald* (Indiana), 30 October 1960, p. 30.

122. Anthony Wickert.
123. 'TV Film Team for Alice Springs,' *The Age*, 14 May 1960, p. 3.
124. 'T.V. Series to be Filmed at Alice Springs.'
125. Anthony Wickert.
126. John Meredyth Lucas, pp. 213–214.
127. Stephen Atkinson, p. 39.
128. Marc Saul.
129. Reg Livermore, Email to Derham Groves, 1 March 2022.
130. Ayanna Thompson, *Blackface*, New York: Bloomsbury Academic, 2021, pp. 53–73.
131. Ibid., pp. 5–18.
132. John Meredyth Lucas, p. 220.
133. Ibid.
134. Michael Terry, *Sand and Sun: Two Gold-Hunting Expeditions with Camels in the Dry Lands of Central Australia*, London: Michael Joseph Ltd., 1937, pp. 206–207.
135. John Meredyth Lucas, p. 221.
136. Ibid.
137. Stephen Vagg, 29 August 2020.
138. 'Spear Misses Star,' *The Age*, 6 April 1961, p. 21.
139. Joan Endress.
140. Kelly Graves.
141. Stephen Vagg, 29 August 2020.
142. Valerie Taylor, *An Adventurous Life*, Sydney: Hachette Australia, 2019, pp. 27–30.
143. Ibid.
144. 'Cast from Abroad: ATN-7 Revue: Stunt Men,' *The Sydney Morning Herald*, 5 February 1961, p. 28.
145. Grahame Ware, Telephone interview with Derham Groves, 2017.
146. Diane Roberts, 'Boy Trains Horses for TV Western,' *The Australian Women's Weekly*, 30 November 1960, p. 4.
147. Grahame Ware.
148. Diane Roberts.
149. Bill Olson.
150. Diane Roberts.
151. Grahame Ware.
152. Ibid.
153. '*Whiplash* Star is Back ... And They Still Remember,' *The Sydney Morning Herald*, 5 April 1974, p. 15.
154. Anthony Wickert.
155. 'Shotgun Guard for *Whiplash* Coach,' *The Sydney Morning Herald*, 17 February 1961, p. 3.

156. "New Western Starting."
157. Joe Finnigan, 'Actor Returns From Abroad, Will Remain,' *The Anderson Herald* (Indiana), 30 October 1960, p. 30.
158. John Meredyth Lucas, pp. 210–211.
159. Ibid.
160. Stephen Vagg, 11 December 2021.
161. 'TV "Town" Will Be Built Near Sydney,' *The Sydney Morning Herald*, 25 August 1959, p. 11.
162. Nan Musgrove, 1 March 1961.
163. Bill Olson.
164. W.R. Olson, 'We Can Be Difficult,' *The Sydney Morning Herald*, 28 May 1960, p. 14.
165. Bill Olson.
166. Ibid.
167. Nan Musgrove, 1 March 1961.
168. Kenneth Brass, 'A Ghost Town in French's Forest Marks the Successful Completion of the *Whiplash* TV series: Australia's "Westerns" are in the Can,' *The Sydney Morning Herald*, 12 February 1961, p. 82.
169. Anthony Wickert.
170. Kate Darian-Smith and David Nichols, '"How Our Forebears Lived": The Modern Nation, Its Folklore and "Living" Heritage in Twentieth-Century Australia,' *Australian Geography*, vol. 49, no. 1 (2018), pp. 199–217.
171. 'ATN-7 Buys Film Studios,' *The Sydney Morning Herald*, 15 July 1960, p. 5.
172. Ibid.
173. "Di," 'Hello! Hello!' *The Sydney Morning Herald*, 19 February 1961, p. 92.
174. Nan Musgrove, 1 March 1961.
175. 'Australian "Western" on CJOH,' *The Ottawa Journal* (Canada), 30 September 1961, p. 62.
176. '"Rich" Adventure Material in Aust.,' *The Sydney Morning Herald*, 20 March 1961, p. 6.
177. Valda Marshall, 'TV Merry-Go-Round: "Li'l Abner" Star on ATN7,' *The Sydney Morning Herald*, 26 February 1961, p. 91.
178. Bob Shiels, 'Bob Shiels on Television: Down Under,' *Calgary Herald* (Canada), 11 November 1961, p. 14.
179. Mimi Mead, 'Biggest Mission: All is Possible to Peter Graves,' *The Star-Gazette* (New York), 22 June 1968, p. 29.
180. Marc Saul.
181. Donald Freeman, 'TV Superspy is a Music Man at Heart,' *The Fort Worth Star Telegram* (Texas), 12 July 1970, p. 127.

Index

A
Aanensen, Peter, 111
  Bellbird (1967–1977), 111
  Jim Bacon, 111
  Sam Green, 112
Aboriginals, ix, 17, 18, 26, 28, 29, 39, 52, 60, 106, 111, 116, 120
  Aboriginal culture, 116
  Aboriginal stockmen, 61
  Bagot Road Native Reserve, 59
  Blackface (2021), 116, 118
  Darwin, 54
  Indigenous magic, 118
  Kipara or "*Wild Turkey*" dance, 30
  Melville Island, 52, 57
  Mamu or "Evil Spirits" dance, 30
  Ngalia, 31
  Ooldea, 27, 31
  Ooldea people, 26, 28, 31
  Tarrawanna (no translation) dance, 30
  Tiwi Island, 52
  Waugaite, 31
Addams, Dawn, 8

Aitken, George, 55
  "Hopalong Cassidy and the Sheep Rustlers" (1954), 56
Aldous, Grant, 72
Alexander, Hal, 11
Alice Springs, 114, 116, 121
  Alice Springs Hotel, 115
  Mparntwe, 114
Allison, June, 9
Andre, Annette, 96, 109, 120, 121
  Cassie, 121
  Fiona Merrick, 120
Angliss, Lady Jacobena, 62, 63
Armbrust, Bill, 54, 85
  "The Coming of Cassidy", 54
Armstrong, Peter, 122
Arness, James, 98
  Gunsmoke (1955–1975), 98, 125, 131
  Matt Dillon, 98
Artransa, 102, 104, 126, 129
Ashton, Queenie, 120
  Mrs. Culbert, 120
Astley, Edwin, 94, 109

Avalon Beach, 98, 99
  Avalon Beach Primary School, 107
Ayers Rock, 114
  Uluru, 114

B
Barker, Jimmy, 26
Barkham, Don, 112, 119
  Link, 112
Barrett, Ray, 130
Bassler, Robert, 3, 5, 7, 8, 19, 28
  Green Grass of Wyoming (1948), 3
Bat Masterson (1958–1961), vii, 104
Bester's Sweets Pty. Ltd., 80
  Hopalong Cassidy Ranch Toffees, 81
"Big" Jim Healey, 53
Bishop, Ron, 103
Bitter Springs (1950), 27, 106
Bonanza (1959–1973), vii, 104, 107
Boomerang, 84, 93
Boone, Richard, 9, 10, 12, 15, 17, 25, 33, 35, 36
  "The Kangaroo", 29
  Gamble, 119
  Have Gun Will Travel, 125
  John W. Gamble, 9, 10, 15, 29
  Paladin, 9
  Red Skies of Montana (1952), 36
Borgnine, Ernest, 11
  "Roo", 11
  Summer of the Seventeenth Doll (1959), 11
Bowie, Jim, 92
Boyd, Fay, 69
Boyd, Grace Bradley, 50, 57, 60, 62, 72
  Hopalong Cassidy: An American Legend (2008), 60
  "Tripalong", 50, 56
  "Trippy", 50

Boyd, Robin, 97
  The Australian Ugliness (1960), 97
Boyd, William, 3, 50, 51, 55, 58, 63, 68, 74, 76, 82, 84
  Borrowed Trouble (1948), 61
  Zephyr, 63
Bromley, Ivor, 118
Brooks, Rand, 61
  "Lucky" Jenkins, 61
Brown, Max, 2, 3, 14, 27, 30, 34
  Wild Turkey (1958), 2, 14, 30, 34
Brownrigg, Blake, 14, 22, 24, 27, 33
Bryant, David, 122
Buffalo Bill Jr. (1955–1956), 107
Bunkhouse Show, The, 70

C
Cadell, John, 118
Chengra, 118
Campion, Jane, xi
  The Power of the Dog (2021), xi
Carr-Glynn, Neva, 110
Cassidy, John, 69
Cattapan, Silvana, 64
Chauvel, Charles, 61
  Jedda (1955), 61, 111
Chauvel, Elsa, 61
Cheyenne (1955–1963), 104, 125
Chin, Ernie, 59
Christie, Robert, 64
Clark, Ross, 75
Clarke, Charles G., 4, 17, 21, 26, 29, 32
  Carousel (1956), 4
  Green Grass of Wyoming, 4
  Miracle on 34th Street (1947), 4
Clavell, James, 103
  King Rat (1962), 103
  Tai-Pan (1966), 103
  The Great Escape (1963), 103
  To Sir with Love (1967), 103

Cleland, Larry, 77
Clune, Frank, 6
Clyde, Andy, 59, 61
 California Carlson, 59
Cobb & Co., ix, 102, 109, 116, 127
Cobb, Chris, 92, 93, 112, 115, 118, 120, 125, 131
Cobb, Christopher "Chris", 92
Cobb, Freeman, 92, 93, 102
Cody, Terence, 56
Cole Brothers Circus, 72
Combo, Clyde, 27
Connolly, Don, 109
Connors, Lily, 70
Cooper, Garry, 9
Cooper, Margaret, 66
Corraberra Station, 28
Courtney, Maude, 10
Cowboys and Indians, vii, 82
Craig, Janette, 110
Craydon, Letty, 12
 Bonaventure, 12
 Kathleen, 12
 Sister Josephine, 12
Creek, Fury, 126–128
Crockett, Davy, 92
Currie, Finlay, 10, 14, 17, 33, 36
 Michael McGuire, 10, 14, 19
 Mudlark, 10

D
Daniels, Geoffrey, 109
Darken, Robert, 121
Darwin, 50, 51, 55
 Darwin Airport, 50–55
 Darwin Primary School, 58, 59
 Darwin Schools, 55–63
 St Mary's Convent, 56
Dawson, Smoky, 38
Day, Gerry, 103, 110
DDT, 24, 25

del Rio, Delores, 102
Denning, Richard, 101
 Dr. Greg Graham, 101
Dingo, Ernie, 52
Disneyland, 128
Dodge, Fred J., 102
Doleman, Guy, 120
 Raike Dartner, 120
Dumpleton, Tom, 72

E
Ealing Studios, 4, 22, 39
Eastman, David, 119
Eastwood, Clint, 104
 Rawhide (1959–1965), 104
Eckersley, Tom, 84
Egan, Ted, 56
Elms, Albert, 109
Endean, John, 19
Endress, Joan, 94, 98, 100, 121
Erskine, Norman, 121
 Cloy, 121
Evans, David, 103

F
Farrar, Willie, 61
 Joe, 61
Faulkner, Chuck, 94, 112
 O'Hara, 112
Fegan, John, 114
 Capart, 114
Field, Daphne, 103, 111
Fink, Harry Julian, 103, 118
 Dirty Harry (1971), 104
Fitchman, Walter, 23
Flanagan, James, 24
Flett, Julian, 114
 Hennessy, 114
Folmer, Frants, 109, 120
Ford, Dale, 114

Ford, John, 8
How Green Is My Valley, 8
Fox, Ben, 93, 104, 108, 111, 128, 130
Code 3 (1957), 108
Freckleton, Peter, 68
Fricker, George, 20
Frontierland, 128
Fry, Susan, 68
Fyna Foods Pty. Ltd., 80
  Hopalong Cassidy Bar 20, 76
  Hoppy Belt Pouch, 76, 80, 81
  Hoppy Chews, 80
  Hoppy Pops, 76
  Hoppy Ringsticks, 80
  Hoppy-Ade, 80

G
Gable, Clark, 9
Gene Autry Show (1950–1955), *The*, 107
Geraghty, Maury, 106, 108, 109
  "The Falcon" (1942–1945), 106
  Whiplash (1948), 107
Gibson, Grace, 102
Ginn, Stewart, 110
Glenwright, Gordon, 118
  Carthy, 118
Goodlet, Ken, 109, 110
  Mike Jacky, 109
Gorge, Ormiston, 114
  Kwartatuma, 114
Gorman, Reg, 110
Gow, Nina, 107
Grade, Lew, 105, 129
  The Adventures of Robin Hood (1955–1960), 94, 106, 107
  Associated Television (ATV), 105, 129
  The Buccaneers (1956–1957), 94, 106, 107
  Independent Television (ITV), 106
  Sir Frances Drake (1961–1962), 108
  William Tell (1958–1959), 106, 107
Graham, Ron, 110
Grant, Cary, 9
Graves, Kelly, 98, 99
Graves, Peter, 92, 96, 97, 102, 106, 110, 113, 117, 125, 126, 130
  The Captains and the Kings (1962), 100
  Fury (1955–1960), 92, 98
  Jim Newton, 92
  Jim Phelps, 101
  Las Vegas Beat (1961), 100
  The Long Grey Line (1955), 92
  The Masque of the Red Death, 108
  Mission Impossible (1966–1973), 101
  Mr. Kingston, 100
  Rogue River (1951), 92
  Stalag 17 (1953), 92
Grayson, Dan, 62
Great Train Robbery (1903), xii
Green, William Ellis, 66
Grey, Richard, 103
Grounds, Roy, 128
Guest, Barbara, 114
Guest, Terry, 75
Gunsmoke (1955–1975), vii

H
Haar, Paul, 65
Hakendorf family, 35
Hall, Colin, 21
Halls of Montezuma, 9
Hardin, Ty, 101
  Bronco (1958–1962), 102
  Moss Andrews, 101
  Riptide (1969), 101

Harris, Keith, 76
Harris, Leslie, 108
 Navy Log (1955–1958), 108
Harris, Tom, 52, 57
 Star Pictures, 60
Hart, Brett, 104, 119
 Bobby, 119
 Mike McKenna, 104
Hartley Stuart-Codde, 24, 38
Have Gun Will Travel
 (1957–1963), vii, 9
Hayes, George, 57, 64
"Windy" Halliday, 57, 64
Hick, John, 62
Hill, Paul, 64
Hopalong Cassidy (1952–1954),
 vii, 125
 Hopalong Cassidy
  Enterprises, 50, 62
 "Hoppy", 50
 Topper, 59, 66, 72, 83
 William Boyd Enterprises, 50
Hopalong Cassidy Game, 76, 79
 Milton Bradley, 79
 W. Owen Pty. Ltd., 78
Hopalong Cassidy good luck token,
 52, 53, 56, 62, 64
Hopalong Cassidy Ranch Toffees, 76
 Bester's Sweets Pty. Ltd., 80
Hopalong Cassidy, ix, 38, 50, 52,
 54, 57, 60, 65, 67, 69, 71,
 76, 85
Hopalong Cassidy's Troopers'
 Creed, 82
Hoppy Cola, 76, 78
 Cosgrove & Co., 77
 Sheekey's Ltd., 77
 W.H. Moyle & Co., 77
Hoskins, Bob, 67
Hotel Darwin, 55
Hugh Gardiner, 64
Hunt, Helen, 67

I
Ifield, Frank, 94
Ingalls, Don, 103, 109, 112,
 121, 126
 Have Gun Will Travel
  (1957–1963), 103
 Solid Gold Brigade, 103
Ivanhoe (1958–1959), 94

J
James W. Steeth & Son, 62
James, Geoff, 56, 59
Jayne, Jennifer, 109
Johnson, Ray, 72
Johnston, Noel, 13
Jolliffe, Eric, 60
Jones, Ian, 13
Jones, Tom, 58, 75
Judd, Noel, 70

K
Kangaroo: The Australian Story
 (1952), ix, 50
 The Australian Story, 2
 The Bushranger, 2
 La Ley del Latigo, 18
 The Land Down Under, 2
 The Law and the Whip, 18
 Loven og Pisken, 18
 The Sundowners, 2
Kangaroos, 5, 16, 17, 21, 27, 28,
 35, 37, 39
Kelly, Jack, 116
 Tjalkalieri, 116
Kemp, Dudley, 14, 16
Kemp, Leilani, 114
Kerr, Deborah, 123
Kilmartin, Leslie, 57
King, Louis, 3
 Green Grass of Wyoming, 3

Kirk, Mark-Lee, 4, 5, 20
  George Washington Slept Here
    (1942), 4
  My Favourite Wife (1940), 4
  Since You Went Away (1944), 4
Kleiner, Harry, 4, 5, 16
Kleiner, Harry, 6
Koala, 16, 104
Konkel, Lou, 26
Koopman, Willi, 114
Kunoth, Ngarla, 61
  Jedda, 61

L
Ladd, Alan, 9
Laramie (1959–1963), 104, 107
Lawford, Peter, 9–11, 13, 15, 17, 25, 31, 33, 35, 36, 38
  Good News (1947), 9
  Richard Connor, 8, 10, 29, 119; Dennis, 15
Lawless, Johnny, 22
Lawson, Thalia, 34
  Bill Welch, 34
Ledward, Dan, 92, 116, 118, 120, 125
Lee, Kendall, 9, 34
Lee, Margo, 110
LeGarde Twins, The, 70, 72
Levy, Jock, 109
Lewin, Ben, 67
  The Dunera Boys (1985), 67
  The Sessions (2012), 67
Leydin, Alice, 52
Leydin, Reg, 53
Lieberman, Leo, 100
Life and Legend of Wyatt Earp (1955–1961), *The*, vii, 125
Livermore, Reg, 117
  "Betty Blockk Buster Follies" (1975), 117
  Maloomba, 117

Lockey, 119
Lone Ranger (1949–1957), *The*, 104
Long, Lionel, 110
Lovell, Nigel, 116
  Edwin Regnor, 116
Lucas, John Meredyth, 121
Lucas, John Meredyth, 99, 108, 111, 115, 119, 120, 126
Lundigan, William, 9
Luton, Lew, 110
Lye, Reg, 120
  Bradley Bradley, 120

M
Maharis, George, 92
  Buz Murdoch, 92
Maples, Terence, 103
Marley, Bob, xii
  "Buffalo Soldier", xii
  "I Shot the Sheriff", xii
Marlowe, Hugh, 9
Martin Berkeley, 5, 6
  Green Grass of Wyoming, 5
Maverick (1957–1962), 104
Maxwell, Peter, 107, 108
McAloon, Claire, 9, 36
McCormick, Joe, 94, 114, 120
  Arnold Lofton, 120
  Lucien Zumwalt, 114
McDermott, Terry, 111
  Frank Bronson, 111
  Homicide (1964–1977), 111
  Jack Sheridan, 112
McDonald, John, 76
McDonnell Rangers, 114, 116
  Tjoritja, 114
McEwin, Scotty, 26
McGuire, Del, 10
McKay, Nell, 13
McKitterick, Steve, 18, 21
McLees, Barney, 66

McLeod, Zelie, 6
Meat Pie Westerns, ix, xii, 106
 Bitter Springs (1950), 12
 The Story of the Kelly Gang (1906), xii
Meikle, Richard, 94
Melbourne, 50, 62, 84
 Melbourne Airport, 76
 Royal Children's Hospital, 63–66
 St George's Catholic Primary School, 64
 Victorian School for Deaf Children, 68–71
 Windsor, 76
 Wirth's Circus, 70–76
 Yooralla, 66
Mickey Mouse, 119
Milestone, Lewis, 3, 6, 9, 12, 15, 16, 19, 25, 31, 34, 38
 All Quiet on the Western Front (1930), 3
 Halls of Montezuma (1951), 3
 Two Arabian Knights (1927), 3
Millard, Oscar, 103, 120
Milner, Martin, 92
 Todd Stiles, 92
Mitchum, Robert, 123
Moore, David, 28
Morrissey, Di, 97, 104
 The Silent Country (2009), 97, 104
Mosick, 31
Mountford, Charles P., 6, 30
Mulford, Clarence E., 50
Mullins, Peter, 109, 127
 Fury Creek, 128
Murdoch, Henry, 27, 116
 Billy Jo, 116

N
Neville, Coralie, 112
 Virginia Jessup, 112

Newland, Simpson, 10
 Paving the Way: A Romance of the Australian Bush (1893), 10
Newton, Dwight, 104, 110
Nichols, Dudley, 3
Nixon, Janice, 69
Noonan, Michael, 101
 The Flying Doctor (1959), 101
 Riptide (1969), 102
North, Loretta, 37
 "Miss Kangaroo", 37
Noy, Arthur Que, 57
NTA Film Network, 92

O
O'Dea, Ernest, 12
O'Hara, Maureen, 7, 8, 10, 13, 14, 17, 24, 25, 31, 33–36, 38
 Bagdad (1949), 35
 Bronwyn, 8, 31, 33, 35
 Del McGuire, 8, 13, 14, 29
 How Green Is My Valley (1941), 7
 Miracle on 34th Street, 7
 Mr. W.C. Price, 33
 Shamrock Lodge., 34
O'Malley, Jack, 14, 15, 36
Official Hopalong Cassidy Trade Mark, 80
 Clement Hack & Co., 80

P
Paddock, Gosch, 71
Parkes, Trevor, 71, 73
Paspalis, Michael, 56
Patience, J.D., 129
Peck, Gregory, 9
Penton, Brian, 6
 Inheritors: A Novel (1936), 6
 Landtakers: The Story of an Epoch (1934), 6

Perry, Lorraine, 71, 73
Peters, Jean, 8
Peterson, Ralph W., 103, 111, 112
 My Name's McGooley, What's Yours?
 (1966–1968), 103
Petrov, Dusya, 53
Petrov, Vladimir, 53
Phynea Paspalis, 56
Pigeon, Walter, 100
Pinchbeck, Mervyn, 13
Pioneer Settlement, 128, 129
Pippen, Gwenda, 116
 Marianne, 116
Plant, Michael, 101, 111, 116
 The Barbara Stanwyck Show
 (1960–1961), 102
 Bourbon Street Beat
 (1959–1960), 102
 The Detectives (1959–1961), 102
Playford, Thomas, 32
Polio, 24, 50, 56, 66
Port Augusta, 4, 11, 15, 17, 20, 21,
 24, 26, 28, 31, 32, 35
 Kurdnatta, 4
 Port Augusta Town Hall, 31, 35
Powell, Moray, 110
Power, Tyrone, 8
 The Mark of Zorro (1940), 8
 Mister Roberts, 9
Price, Will, 8
Pym, Walter, 110

R

Rafferty, Chips, 12, 14, 27, 33, 106,
 112, 113
 Bitter Springs (1950), 112
 The Desert Rats (1956), 112
 Mutiny on the Bounty (1962), 112
 The Overlanders (1946), 112
 Sorrel, 112
 The Sundowners (1960), 112, 123

Trooper "Len" Leonard, 12, 14
Raine, Norman Reilly, 5
 The Adventures of Robin Hood
 (1938), 5
Ramsay, Doug, 14
Rank, J. Arthur, 8
Reichenbach, Herbert, 27
Reiman, Eric, 118
 Morgan, 118
 Walt Sullivan, 118
Restless Gun (1957–1959), *The*, 104
Reynall, Paul
 Joe, 61
Roberts, Kay, 104
Robertson, Dale, 102
 Jim Hardie, 102
 Tales of Wells Fargo, 104
Roddenberry, Gene, 93, 104,
 113, 120
 Helen of Abajinian, 104
 Star Trek (1966–1969), 104
Rogers, Ginger, 97
 Pink Jungle (1959), 97
Root, Wells, 104
Ross, Phillip, 119
 Joe Pearce, 119
Rouse, Allan, 64
Route 66 (1960–1964), 92, 94
Roy Rogers Show (1951–1957),
 The, 125
Royal Children's Hospital, 63, 65
Rymill, Arthur, 24

S

Salk, Jonas, 66
Savoy Corporation Ltd, 126
Scheuer, Stanley, 26
Schneider, Wendy, 16
Searl, Geoff, 100
Secombe, John, 64
Seipelt, Mary, 13

77 Sunset Strip (1958–1964), 130
Shand, Ron, 110
Shawn, Ted, 31
Sherman, Harry "Pop", 50
Simmons, Jean, 8
Simpson Desert, 120
Simpson, Colin, 28, 30
Sinclair, W., 85
Smart, Ralph, 106, 108
Smith, Constance, 8
  The 13th Letter (1951), 8
Snody, Robert, 4–7, 12, 33, 34, 36
Spaghetti Westerns, vii, xii
  A Fist Full of Dollars (1964), vii–ix
  Once Upon a Time in the West (1967), ix
  The Good, the Bad, and the Ugly (1966), ix
Spiegle, Dan, 62
St Leon, Leo, 71, 73
Stabler, Robert, 53, 56, 63
Star Pictures, 52, 56, 57, 61
Stevens, Mark, 9
SUGA, xi
  "That That", xi
Sugarfoot (1957–1961), 125

T
Tales of the Texas Rangers (1955–1959), vii
Tales of Wells Fargo (1957–1962), vii, 102, 125
Taronga Park Zoo, 12, 37
  Edward J. Hallstrom, 37
Tate, John, 114
  Oscar Wenders, 114
Taylor, Grant, 118, 121
  John Dundee, 118
  John Kerrabee, 121
Taylor, Ron, 122
Taylor, Valerie, 122

Teale, Leonard, 120
  Norton "Teddy Bear" Culbert, 120
Templeton, Bill, 116
Templeton, William, 104
Terra nullius, 28
Terry, Michael, 119
Tierney, Roger, 27
Tim Tam, 82
  Nathalie Sanchez, 83
Tingwell, Charles, 12, 16, 27, 33, 70
  Matt, 12, 16
Tipperary Tilipoura, 56
Tjunkata "Nosepeg" Tjupurrula, 112
  John Carter, 112
Tolmer, Alex, 62
Tombstone Territory (1957–1960), 104, 125
Tonks, Greg, 59
Topper, 72, 77, 80, 85
Toyoshima, Hajime, 57
Tudawali, Robert, 61, 111, 116, 119
  Dalgowlie, 111, 116
  Kogarah, 111
  Kuanspa, 111
  Kuraba, 111
  Marbuck, 61, 111
  Mundaru, 111
  Roonga, 111, 119

U
Ulungura, Matthias, 57

V
Vegemite, 82
  Alan Weeks, 82
  Craig Noyce, 82
  "Happy Little Vegemites" (1954), 82
Ventura, S.S., 53
Vic Streatham, 59

Victorian School for Deaf Children, 63, 68, 69
The Deaf Children's Chronicle, 69
Emerald A. Goetze, 70
G.E. Hansford, 70
Virginian, The, 107

W
Wagon Train (1957–1965), vii, 104, 125
Wagstaff, Stuart, 113
  Lieutenant Hoffman, 113
Walley, Richard, 52
Walshe, Keith, 70
Walt Disney, 85
  Davy Crockett, King of the Wild Frontier (1955), 85
Ware, Grahame, 123
Ware, Lionel, 123
Waterhole, Wigley, 121
Waters, John, 59
Watt, Nate, ix, 16
  Borderland (1937), 16
  Hopalong Cassidy Returns (1936), 16
  Law of the Pampas (1939), 16
Wayne, Pat, 59
Weaver, Dennis, 131
  Chester, 131
Welch, Bettina, 110
Wells Fargo, ix, 102
Wenban, Eric, 25
West Melbourne Stadium, 71
West, Morris, 103
  The Devil's Advocate (1959), 103
  The Shoes of the Fisherman (1963), 103
West, Wild, 7, 84
Westbrook, Eric, 128
Westbrook, Ian, 71
Westenhiser, George, 16, 23–25, 36
  Cherry Wheatley, 36

Whelan, Ron, 114
Whiplash (1960–1961), ix, 92, 94
  "The Actress", 104, 109
  "The Adelaide Arabs", 103, 112
  "A Dilemma in Wool", 103
  "Act of Courage", 104, 110
  "Barbed Wire", 104, 111, 118
  "The Bone That Whispered", 111, 116
  "The Canoomba Affair", 103
  "Convict Town", 110
  "Dark Runs the Sea", 97, 120
  "The Day of the Hunter", 103, 112
  "Dutchman's Reef", 104, 111, 120
  "Episode in Bathurst" (1961), 93, 97, 104, 109
  "Fire Rock", 111
  "The Hunters", 103, 111
  "The Legacy", 116
  "Love Story in Gold", 103
  "The Magic Wire", 103, 111
  "Ribbons and Wheels", 103
  "Rider on the Hill", 104, 118
  "Sarong", 104, 113
  "The Secret of the Screaming Hills", 103
  "The Solid Gold Brigade", 107, 109
  "Stage Fright", 103
  "Storm River", 97, 103, 121, 122
  "The Wreckers", 111
White, Don, 59
Wickert, Anthony, 92, 96, 104, 109–111, 125
  Dan Ledward, 109
Wild West Show, The, 125
Williams, Delia, 118
  Helen Tanner, 118
William Ellis Green (WEG), 66, 72
Windsor Hotel, 63, 68
Winfield, Joan, 99
Wirth's Circus, 70, 71, 76
  The Bunkhouse Concert, 70

Wise, Charles, 21
Wise, Frank, 56
Wise, Ken, 63
Wolveridge, Charles, 109
Woodruff, Harold A., 6
Woolundunga Station,
   20, 23, 25
  Mrs E.J. Farrell, 20
  Rooloora, 20
Wrather, Jack, 105
  Lassie (1954–1974), 105, 107
  The Lone Ranger, 105
Wurtzel, Paul, 20

X
Xiao Wang, 84

Y
Yooralla, 66, 68

Z
Zanuck, Darryl F., 3, 7, 8, 33, 38
Zanuckville, 32, 33, 36, 39
  Hollywood Park, 33
  Shamrock Lodge, 33

CPSIA information can be obtained
at www.ICGtesting.com
Printed in the USA
LVHW081326050323
740957LV00007B/1060